SCRIPTU

A Dialog between John Bapstead and Martin Childfont

IS INFANT BAPTISM SCRIPTURAL?

IS BAPTISM AN ACT OF GOD OR OF MAN?

BAPTISM AND REGENERATION.

HOW OLD IS THE BAPTISTIC DOCTRINE?

IMMERSION OR SPRINKLING?

IS IT TRUE THAT A PERSON ONCE SAVED IS ALWAYS SAVED?

by

UURAS SAARNIVAARA, Ph.D., Th.D.

Wipf and Stock Publishers
EUGENE, OREGON

Wipf and Stock Publishers
199 West 8th Avenue, Suite 3
Eugene, Oregon 97401

Scriptural Baptism
A Dialog Between John Bapstead and Martin Childfont
By Saarnivaara, Uuras
ISBN: 1-59244-249-8
Publication date: May, 2003
Previously published by Vantage Press, January, 1953 .

Preface
by Dr. Rod Rosenbladt

As writers, theologians are hardly "top o' the heap!" We theologians tend to churn out works that are absent of skilled use of analogy, devoid of concretes, and often tedious and dreary to read. We do not represent the Holy and Gracious Christ well in our use of language. We write books that may be "on the side of the angels" theologically, but which are still in many ways, bad books. Lay theologian C.S. Lewis "stands out like a sore thumb" in his exposition of Christianity. His books are not just well thought out and well argued. They are expressed with a linguistic beauty that many would say was impossible when writing in the field of theology. (And, I think, the more Christian books a person had read, the more impossible it would seem!) C.S. Lewis is read by curious non-Christians more than any other Christian writer, and for more than one reason (see Richard Purtill's *C.S.Lewis's Case for the Christian Faith)* First, Lewis writes of Christianity without trying to "trim its edges" so that no one will be upset by what it claims. The Christianity of which he writes is robust and Creedal – not the soft "Christianity-and-water" we so often hear today. Second, Lewis is a thoroughgoing supernaturalist, willing to defend the superiority of Christian supernaturalism over the vapidity and flatness of twentieth-century humanist, materialist alternatives. But thirdly, he never, never hid behind "Christian language" – as if the repetition of pious Christian phrases amounted to a defense. Lewis found normal English sufficient to explain what were sometimes very difficult concepts. He once remarked that if you cannot explain your Chalcedonian Christology to the blue collar worker in East London, then you do not yet clearly understand your position!

Once in a while, a Christian thinker writes a work that is not just "roundly and soundly Biblical," but is attractive to the reader as well, a book that sort of invites you to read it. There can be a variety of reasons that an author's writing is attractive as writing. Those more literate than I see in the poetry of a Browning or a Milton or the glorious exposition of a Dante a beauty that seems forever hidden from my eyes. I might "best" such people in a chemistry or biology laboratory, but in the field of literature they will "best me" any day of the week. They are much more able than I to see and understand literature as literature. But once in a while there is a Christian book that invites people like me to read it *because of its form.* One of the several reasons a Christian book can be attractive as writing is that it deals well with an important issue *in a form that is unexpected.*

When most Christians think of a book on Holy Baptism or the Lord's Supper, we immediately imagine massive, forbidding tomes written by and for theologians. Of course, there are exceptions such as the sort of thing Inter-Varsity Press published back in its better days. I think immediately of, for example, Bridges and Phypers' *The Water That Divides* (a survey of what positions Christians have held with regard to Baptism, the history of the movement, the Scriptures on which they based their view(s), the arguments the group marshaled for its view, etc.) Similarly, the same authors' *Holy Communion: The Meal That Unites?* published in England by Hodder & Stoughton. Such works are of inestimable value to Christians who are new to the faith, and who are immediately confronted with a plethora of different denominational claims with regard to the Sacraments. Why? Because books like these, in a simple and straightforward way, introduce to the new Christian "the basics" concerning doctrines that have caused so much contention in Christian history. For this reason alone, such books are attractive to readers. Their "form" is the form of simple introduction to complex material.

U. Saarnivaara's *Scriptural Baptism* is noteworthy for similar reasons. As with the old Inter-Varsity books, it has the form of a simple introduction to a complex subject. But its style or form is noteworthy for another reason. It is written in the form of a living conversation. A Lutheran of the old, classical variety and a Scripturally-knowledgeable Baptist are having a discussion of the doctrine of Baptism. Undergirding the whole book is, thank God, the knowledge so absent in our day, that logically, both positions could be in error, but that it is impossible that both positions could be simultaneously and under the same conditions, true! In other words, their position is utterly unlike the postmodernists' anxious strategy of today. The two men are in disagreement over what Holy Baptism is, over what it promises to give (if anything), and over who the proper subjects of Holy Baptism are. The Lutheran is defending what theologians call "baptismal regeneration" and argues that infants are truly and Scripturally proper recipients of Holy Baptism. He believes that simple water, comprehended and connected with the Word of God actually gives to the child the benefits of Christ's death for him or her. By simple water connected to God's Word of promise, the infant is "born again." His Baptist friend, of course, disagrees. He defends the much more common and popular view of "believers-only baptism." Thus, the book's set up.

The method the two men employ is the same method we find in the New Testament, the method employed by the Lord Jesus in conflict with his contemporaries and the method consistently employed by His Apostles, that is, the marshaling of Biblical passages which speak to the point at issue. Unlike today's conversations which almost never rise above the level of whether something doctrinal "is practical" or "really works," the two characters in *Scriptural Baptism* never vary from the real conversation. And the real conversation is, "Which of these views (if either) is true?" Many Christian readers will very quickly be "drawn in" to this conversation for the simple reason that they have had this conversation with others – or, if not with someone on the other side, then within their own inner wonderings.

For those who have the knee-jerk reaction, "Well, what about the context of the verses?" there is discussion of that alongside the verses. For those who "just know" the right position *a priori,* there is challenge ("And how is it that you 'just know' your position is the sound one?") For those who are genuinely curious, there are Biblical passages quoted which just might not yet figure as part of their thinking – new evidence as it were. For those who have heard only one side of the argument, Saarnivaara's book is helpful in presenting the opposite side argued well – something every well-educated person should know. My Baptist friends will howl at this, claiming that "John Bapstead" plays a part something like Thrysimicus played to Socrates in Plato's *Republic.* But then again, if it were not for Martin Childfont's able replies, would they not own the arguments as their own?

I commend this re-issue of *Scriptural Baptism* by Wipf & Stock Publishers and hope that it has a wide audience. My own denominational publishing house in its infinite wisdom dropped it (along with a whole series of Lutheran classics) for reasons I do not know. But this is a unique book, and one badly needed by those new to the Reformation – especially young couples who have recently had a baby! I can't count the number of copies of this little book I have mailed out to evangelical couples who, for most of their lives, have never considered anything but that they would have their children "dedicated" after they were born. Then, by listening to the White Horse Inn, they began to wonder whether there might be justification for what Reformation people call "Sacraments." Many in our day, beginning to be drawn to the Reformation, face the issue of Holy Baptism in just such a "non-theoretical" way – having a new baby!

This simple volume can be of inestimable help in answering the questions Scripturally. It is filled with Scripture texts, two sides are disagreeing and each is saying why. And the book can be read and understood by non-technicians of theology.

Foreword

The doctrine of Christian baptism has been a subject of dispute for many centuries. This question divides Christianity into two large sections: the churches which practice infant baptism and the churches which reject it and follow the principle that baptism is to be administered to those, and to those only, who have experienced and professed saving faith in Christ at an age of discretion. Although much literature has been published on both sides, there still are numerous people who desire more light on this problem.

The writer of this book believes that God's word in the Holy Scriptures is the supreme and only norm and rule of doctrine, life and practice in the Christian Church. The Church has no right to modify or dispense with the teachings of the Bible, particularly of the New Testament. At this point both pedobaptists (those who practice infant baptism) and antipedobaptists (those who oppose infant baptism) are on common ground.

The literary form of discussion, or dialog, has been used many times in dealing with the doctrine of baptism. Sometimes books of this type have been criticized on the grounds that the same person is speaking all the time, giving both the arguments and counterarguments. In order to avoid such criticism—which is largely justified—all the main arguments against infant baptism and for the baptistic doctrine of baptism in this book are taken from Baptist literature, particularly from books that Bible-believing Baptists recommend as fairly representative of their position.

The Baptist view of baptism is held by many other groups or denominations, the Pentecostals, Adventists, Jehovah's Witnesses, etc. The term *baptistic*, with a small initial, is used in this book to describe the view common to these various groups, while the term *Baptist* is used when the Baptist denomination is meant.

The writer hopes and prays that the discussions in this book will lead some Christians to a better understanding of the Biblical doctrine of baptism, and to obedience of the faith once delivered unto the saints.

UURAS SAARNIVAARA
Hancock, Michigan, February, 1953

Contents

Introduction

Martin Childfont and John Bapstead were neighbors in the city of Zion. The former was a member of a church that practiced infant baptism. The latter belonged to a church that taught that baptism is the immersion or dipping of a person in water, on confession of faith in Christ, administered in the name of the Father, Son, and Spirit.[1]

Martin and John had originally been members of the same church, and both of them had been baptized as infants. But John had become converted to the faith of those who opposed infant baptism, whereas Martin had come to a personal faith and knowledge of Christ as his Savior in his own church. For a while he too had struggled with doubts about infant baptism; but his study of the Scriptures and literature on baptism had led him to the conviction that the baptism that he had received in his infancy was a Biblical baptism, and that he did not need to be baptized anew.

John and Martin had occasionally exchanged opinions on baptism. But one night they decided to discuss the subject more thoroughly. Although their conversation lasted several hours, they were unable to reach a conclusion and agreed to continue it the next day. John starts the actual discussion.

John Bapstead: You remember, Martin, the time when we both were members of your church. You also remember how I left it and joined the congregation of which I am now a member. The reason was that the Lord led me to a new understanding of His will concerning baptism. I wanted to obey His word and to have a Scriptural baptism. It was not easy to sever the ties that bound me to the church of my childhood and youth, and to join another church. But I had to do it in order to be obedient to the Lord, and He always blesses those who do. Since that time I have hoped and prayed that God would also reveal to you His will concerning baptism. As you know, we reject infant baptism because it is without warrant, either express or implied, in the Scripture. First, there is no express command that infants should be baptized. Second, there is no clear example of the baptism of infants. Third,

---

[1] Edward T. Hiscox, *The New Directory for Baptist Churches* (Philadelphia: American Baptist Publication Society, 1894), p. 123.

the passages held to imply infant baptism contain, when fairly interpreted, no reference to such a practice.[1]

Martin Childfont: It's nice that you have such an affectionate concern for me. Before we start our discussion on baptism, we should agree on the principles of the interpretation of the Scriptures. You stated that there are passages in Scripture which are held to imply infant baptism, but that those passages contain no reference to such a practice when fairly interpreted. We should have a common understanding of the "fair interpretation" of God's word. Will you accept as a basic principle of fair interpretation the old statement: if the plain and obvious literal sense make good sense, seek no other sense?

John: I will. I believe that all sound interpretation of Scripture should follow that principle.

Martin: Will you also accept the principle that the Bible must be used as its own interpreter, so that passages which are not clear in themselves must be interpreted with the help of other Scriptural passages which speak of the same thing?

John: I think that that principle is also sound as a fair interpretation of the Bible.

Martin: Fine. We are getting off to a good start in our conversation. When we study the Scriptures, it may happen that there appears to be a discrepancy between its statements and the teachings of the church, or the denomination to which we belong. There are people who in practice, though perhaps not in expressed statements, think: "Scripture is right since it is God's word, and we are right because our doctrine is true. If, therefore, a Scriptural statement seems to be in conflict with our doctrine, it must be interpreted in harmony with the latter." Do you in any way agree with that principle?

John: No, certainly not. Who are those who follow such an impossible principle?

Martin: The majority of churches and denominations seem to be. A large amount of theological work is done according to that principle, although it may not be expressed, or even admitted. But I think that we should be on our guard primarily in *our own* case, lest *we* follow that deceptive principle. Let us take care that we remove the beam first from our own eye, and then see how we can take the mote from our brother's. We all have a strong tendency to follow that erroneous principle without being

[1] Augustus Hopkins Strong, *Systematic Theology* (5th ed., revised and enlarged; New York: A. C. Armstrong and Son, 1896), p. 535.

aware of it—but we have a rather sharp eye that sees when our brother follows it.

John: I admit that you are right with regard to that danger. The Bible should be the supreme and only source and norm of our faith and life, not only in principle but also in practice.

Martin: We agree, then, on this point. Scripture should be understood and interpreted according to its obvious literal sense, whenever it makes good sense, and it should be used as its own interpreter. Our confession of faith and doctrine must be corrected according to the word of God and not the Bible according to the doctrine of our church. There is, however, one more question that requires an answer, namely, the question of the use of reason in the interpretation of the Scriptures. Your remark about a "fair interpretation" seems to imply this problem. I think we agree on the principle that human reason and its conclusions should never be placed above the statements of Scripture. If there appears to be conflict between the Bible and our reason, or the apparent results of human science, psychology, and such, in questions pertaining to the Christian faith, we should follow the Bible, not human reason, psychology or science. Do you agree with me on that point?

John: I do. If we were to follow our reason, human science, psychology, and such, we would be rationalists and not Christians.

Martin: Well, it's fine that we find ourselves in concord on this question. I think that human reason has its legitimate and necessary place in the interpretation of Scripture and theology, for it is the means by which we humans perceive and think. When God speaks to us in His word He uses human language, and thus He follows logic and grammar, for otherwise we could not understand what He means. The Holy Spirit is logical and grammatical in speaking to us through the men who have written the Scriptures. The Bible and Christian faith are logical and in that sense reasonable. All fair interpretation of Scripture should therefore be grammatical and logical. Anyone who errs in grammar cannot but err also in this doctrine. All interpretation of the Bible which is in conflict with the simple rules of grammar and logic must be wrong. Do you accept this principle?

John: Of course, I do. How could we ever know what the Scriptural text means if we did not take it in its simple grammatical sense, when that sense makes good sense?

Martin: Would you accept as good sense a grammatical sense that runs against natural human reason and psychology?

John: I would, for the natural reason of man cannot understand the things of God. Our reason must be enlightened by the Holy Spirit in order to understand the truth and will of God.

Martin: Would you substitute in any question a so-called enlightened reason, sometimes known as Christian consciousness, Christian experience, or Christian conviction for the word of God in its simple grammatical sense?

John: No, I would not. Being Bible-believing Christians we should follow the word of God. Our reason, Christian consciousness, experience, and conviction must be brought into harmony with the Scriptures, and not *vice versa.*

Martin: One more question. There are many things on which the Bible says nothing but which still belong to Christianity, or at least are necessary things in the life of the Church. For instance, the New Testament never speaks of women having participated in holy communion; neither does it speak of Sunday schools, church edifices, of the use of automobiles for going to church. Do you think that the Church has a right to have these things, and also to regard them as being in harmony with the will of God, although they are not mentioned in the Bible?

John: Of course, I do. In whatever thing the Bible gives no commandment or instruction, we are free, if only it is in harmony with the spirit of the word of God.

Martin: Do you think that a thing is in harmony with the spirit of God's word if it can be logically deduced from its plain statements, although it is not expressly stated?

John: I do. For instance, although women are never mentioned as having participated in holy communion, we may deduce it from the fact that it is never forbidden, and that, according to the teachings of the New Testament, there is neither man nor woman, but all are one in Christ.

Martin: Fine. Let us remember these principles in our discussion on baptism.

John: One more remark. Some pedobaptists admit that there is neither clear precept nor example in the New Testament to commend the practice of infant baptism. They hold, nevertheless, that the general spirit of the Gospel favors it. Fundamental truths are taught there, and from them the practice may be inferred.[1] I think that by basing our doctrine and practice on what we regard as the general spirit or scope of Scripture, we are able to prove anything and to regard any doctrine as Scriptural. I believe that every doctrine must be based on the plain and clear statements of Scriptures. We know the "spirit" of Scripture only from its plain statements.

---

[1] Hiscox, *op. cit.,* p. 486.

Martin: I am in complete agreement with you on that point, too. All the falsifiers of Christianity have used that trick: the men who have originated or developed it have replaced the plain teachings of the word of God in its simple grammatical sense with what they have thought to be its "spirit" or "general scope."

Since we agree on the principles of the interpretation of Scripture, and on the Bible as the source and norm of the Christian truth, let us turn to the discussion of the problem of infant baptism.

SCRIPTURAL BAPTISM

A Dialog between John Bapstead
and Martin Childfont

I. Infant Baptism

John Bapstead: The question of infant baptism is the main point of dissension between you and me. As I have already stated, infant baptism is without warrant, either express or implied, in the Scriptures. There is no express command that infants should be baptized, nor is there any clear example of the baptism of infants. The passages held to imply infant baptism contain, when fairly interpreted, no reference to such practice.

1. CIRCUMCISION AND BAPTISM.

Martin Childfont: I remember that statement of yours. You say that there are no passages in the Bible which imply infant baptism. We believe that one group of such passages implying infant baptism are those speaking of circumcision and baptism.

John: I know that in your doctrine infant baptism has taken the place of circumcision under the Abrahamic covenant. To this we reply that the view contradicts the New Testament idea of the Church, by making it an hereditary body, in which fleshly birth, and not the new birth, qualifies for membership. The fair understanding of this matter is that just as the national Israel typified the spiritual Israel, so the circumcision which immediately followed, not preceded natural birth, bids us baptize children, not before but after spiritual birth. The Christian Church is either a natural, hereditary body, or it was merely typified by the Jewish people. In the former case, baptism belongs to all children of Christian parents, and the Church is indistinguishable from the world. In the latter case, it belongs only to spiritual descendants, and therefore only to true believers.[1] *

Martin: I agree with most of your thoughts in that statement. It is true that the Christian Church is not a hereditary body. It is a spiritual body in which the new birth alone qualifies for membership. We too believe that the Christian Church is the communion of saints in which the Gospel is rightly taught, and the sacraments administered according to the institution of Christ.

---

* All references are appended to the chapters in which they are cited.

1

It is composed of believers, saints, sheep who hear and follow their master's voice.[2] I also agree with you that the Christian Church is merely typified by the people of Israel, for Paul speaks of the "natural Israel" and the "Israel of God," or the Christian Church.[3]

Let us start from the Scriptural idea which you stated, that the natural Israel typified the spiritual Israel, the Israelitic nation the Christian Church.

In making His covenant with Abraham, God commanded him to take the sign of circumcision. He was an old man when he took this sign. It was to him, as Paul says, a seal of the righteousness of faith that he had before he was circumcised.[4] First, he had the justifying faith. Then he received the sign of the covenant as a seal of the righteousness of faith. The order of events was right, according to your way of thinking. But the children of his household were to be circumcised at the age of eight days, that is, those who were not already older. Thus, although circumcision was a sign of the righteousness of faith that Abraham had before the sign itself, the same sign was also given to the infants. God wanted to make them partakers of the privileges of His covenant in their early infancy. What do you say to that, brother John?

John: What you say of circumcision is simple Biblical truth, and I have nothing special to say about that. But it does not apply to baptism, for it did not come in the place of circumcision. Baptism has no connection with, and no reference to, circumcision whatever. If baptism, a Christian ordinance, were designed to take the place of circumcision, which was a Mosaic rite, wouldn't Christ have so stated, or the apostles have mentioned the fact? But no allusion is to be found to any such design. Circumcision was an external sign of an external union with a national congregation, to secure the separation of the Jews from all other nations and races, and their unity as a people. Baptism is an external sign of an inward spiritual work of grace already wrought in the heart. It indicates not the separation of races, but the unity of the true people of God, of all races, as believers in Christ, without distinction of blood or tongue. Jewish Christians for a time insisted on the practice of both circumcision and baptism, which proves they did not understand the one to have displaced the other.[5]

Martin: I did not state that baptism has taken the place of circumcision. But we have reason to make an investigation into the question whether baptism has any connection with, or any reference to, circumcision. Let's see what Paul says on the matter. "In whom (Christ) ye were also circumcised with a circumcision not made with hands, in the putting off of the body of the flesh, in the circumcision of Christ; having been buried with him in baptism, wherein ye were also raised with him through faith." [6] Paul calls baptism the circumcision of Christ. How can you say that baptism has no reference to circumcision?

John: I admit that my statement was too categorical. According to those words of Paul, there is some kind of analogy between circumcision and baptism.

Martin: There is another part of your statement that needs correction. You said that circumcision was a Mosaic rite. A short while ago we discussed it as a rite of the Abrahamic covenant. Did you forget that?

John: I was ill-advised in those words too, following Hiscox. It did not occur to me that this statement of Hiscox was wrong.

Martin: It is quite usual that we follow authorities without examining the correctness of their statements. Circumcision was not a part of the Mosaic covenant but of the Abrahamic covenant. Thus it had a much larger application than the former. It was closely connected with justification by faith and the promise of the coming Savior.

You said that since the Jewish Christians for a time insisted on the practice of both circumcision and baptism, the latter could not displace the former. Do you think that the Jewish Christians were right in this insistence of theirs, or was it based on error—in other words, was their attitude in harmony with the plan of God, or was it in conflict with it?

John: The Jewish Christians were, of course, in error. Otherwise Christian Jews should be circumcised even now.

Martin: Does an erroneous notion and practice prove anything?

John: I guess not. I accepted that argument of Hiscox without considering the fact that an erroneous idea proves nothing.

Martin: You said that circumcision was an external sign of an external union with a national congregation, to secure the separation of the Jews from all other nations, and their unity as a people. In saying so you forgot that circumcision was not a part of the Mosaic covenant, and was therefore not limited to Israel. The various nations which descended from Abraham used it, and not only Israel. But that is of little significance for us in our discussion. In a certain sense it is true that circumcision intended to secure the separation of Israel from other nations and to unite them as God's people. But it seems to me that in these very respects there is an analogy between circumcision and baptism.

Doesn't baptism, too, intend to secure the separation of God's people from the people of this world, and to unite them?

John: Of course, it does. There seems to be an analogy between circumcision and baptism in these respects. Unfortunately baptism has served to separate the various groups of God's people in the New Covenant, instead of uniting them. But that is due to the Christians' failure to follow the Biblical teaching of baptism, not to baptism itself.

Martin: You are right in what you said. The very purpose of our discussion is to find out what the word of God really teaches on baptism, in order that one baptism should unite us too, as brothers.

According to your view, circumcision was an external sign of an external union with a national congregation, whereas baptism is an external sign of an inward spiritual grace already wrought in the heart. Do you think that, also, in the case of Abraham, circumcision was such an external sign of his belonging to a national congregation? Wasn't it, as Paul says, a seal of the righteousness of grace which Abraham had before circumcision? And wasn't the righteousness of faith an inward grace wrought in the heart?

John: Of course, it was. But wasn't circumcision also, as I said, an external sign of an external union with a national congregation?

Martin: Abraham was the first man ever to be circumcised. Don't you think that his circumcision was the pattern of the significance of that rite?

John: I think you are right there. I had never thought of it from that point of view.

Martin: You admit, then, that circumcision, too, was an external sign of an inward spiritual grace. This is obvious also from the fact that circumcision was the sign of the covenant which included the promise "to be a God unto thee and to thy seed after thee." [7] The profit of the circumcision was, as Paul says, that "they were intrusted with the oracles of God." [8] God's promise to be their God and His word certainly meant much more than a mere external union with a national congregation.

I am sure you have read how Moses emphasized that mere external circumcision was not enough. A circumcision of the heart was needed in order that the Israelites be true people of God. "Circumcise therefore the foreskin of your hearts, and be not stiffnecked." [9] Another time Moses promised, "The Lord thy God will circumcise thine heart, and the heart of thy seed, to love the

Lord thy God with all thine heart." [10] Jeremiah [11] and Apostle Paul [12] also speak of the circumcision of the heart as the spiritual meaning and fulfillment of the rite of circumcision. Don't you see, brother John, that the entire Bible teaches circumcision as an external sign of an internal grace?

John: Well, I must again concede that you are right and that I haven't been careful enough in studying and considering this matter.

Martin: The inward spiritual grace that circumcision signified was a renewal of the heart to faith, love to God, and willing obedience to Him. When Paul deals with the question of circumcision he shows that although it required faith, and some people were faithless, the covenant remained in force on God's side. It was broken only on the part of men. "For what if some were without faith? shall their want of faith make of none effect the faithfulness of God?" [13]

The words show that God's covenant and His faithfulness to it were unchanging and objectively valid realities, but men could enjoy the blessings of the covenant only through a personal faith and obedience. Its subjective blessings depended on faith. In the case of Abraham the personal prerequisite, namely, faith, preceded the rite, but otherwise the inward circumcision or renewal to faith and obedience followed afterward.

John: I must admit again that your explanation seems to follow the statements of the Bible.

Martin: You admitted some time ago that circumcision and baptism are analogous, since Paul calls baptism the circumcision of Christ, or Christian circumcision. In the case of Abraham, circumcision was a seal of the righteousness of faith that he had before this rite. It corresponds to the baptism of people who are converted before baptism, as Cornelius and his household were, and as often happens even in our time. But most Israelites received circumcision as infants; when they reached the age of discretion they had to appropriate its blessings and fulfill its requirements afterward, although the majority of them never did so. Here circumcision is analogous to infant baptism. Isn't it, brother John?

John: I cannot deny that it is. But a mere analogy doesn't suffice to establish a Christian doctrine.

Martin: You are right; a mere analogy is not enough here. But I wish to add one more thought on the relationship between circumcision and baptism. Paul calls baptism the circumcision of Christ, and an undeniable fact is that, according to the plan of

God, the use of circumcision was to cease when the use of baptism started in its full Christian sense after Pentecost. You deny that baptism took the place of circumcision. Nevertheless, in my view that thought is implied in the two facts that I mentioned. I cannot, of course, force you to follow my line of thought, but in my view this logic is inescapable.

John: I see now that the idea of baptism in the place of circumcision can be defended with the Bible. I can no longer oppose it categorically, as I did at the outset.

Martin: I am glad to see that you are willing to admit facts, even when they are in conflict with your former views. You probably think that God's attitude toward infants in the New Covenant isn't the same as it was in the Old Covenant. Am I right?

John: Well, I think you are. The two covenants are so different that although circumcision was to be given to infants, baptism should not be given to babes who do not understand what is spoken and done to them.

Martin: Although there are differences between the Old and New Covenants, there are also similarities. They are analogous in many respects, not only with regard to circumcision and baptism. These correspondences are due to the fact that the New Covenant is not absolutely new, but is built on the foundation of the Old Covenant. The entire Old Covenant was preparatory to the New Covenant. In both covenants men were saved by grace alone, through faith, and in both of them believers had to show their faith by love and obedience. Or do you think that Abraham, David, and the other saints of the Old Covenant were saved by works, and not by grace, through faith?

John: Of course not. The two covenants are similar in that respect.

Martin: A difference was that the Old Covenant people put their trust in the coming Savior, whereas the New Covenant people put their trust in the Savior who has come. The Holy Spirit worked in the Old Covenant, but He was not given to dwell in the hearts of believers in the same sense as in the New Covenant. But we are discussing God's attitude toward infants. Let's turn to that question in the New Covenant.

2. Proselyte Baptism and the Baptism of Families.

Martin (continues): In order to have a proper historical "context" for our discussion of the attitude of Christ and the Apostolic

Church toward children, we should know something of the so-called proselyte baptism.

You probably know that proselytes were Gentile converts to Judaism, or to the religion of Israel. The Old Covenant was never exclusively national, limited to the descendants of Jacob. It was primarily a religious covenant, and people who accepted the religion of Israel became its fullfledged members. At the time of Christ, the Jews were missionary-minded in the extreme, particularly the Pharisees and scribes. They "compassed sea and land to make one proselyte," as Christ says.[14] Three things were required of those who became "proselytes of righteousness" or "perfect Israelites" in every respect: circumcision of men, baptism and sacrifice of all, both men and women. The rabbinic literature deals so much with the proselyte baptism that a sizable book could be made if all the statements were gathered together. This baptism was used already before Christ, and during His public ministry it was practiced wherever Gentiles were converted to Judaism.

John: Some authorities say that the proselyte baptism did not exist among the Jews before the time of Christ, and others hold that the whole thing is uncertain.[16]

Martin: I know that's what you find in a large section of baptistic literature. But you have perhaps some confidence in Doctor Strong, who was one of the leading Baptist theologians of the nineteenth century. He quotes the following passage from Alfred Edersheim's book *Life and Times of Jesus the Messiah:* "We have positive testimony that the baptism of proselytes existed in the time of Hillel and Shammai. For, whereas the school of Shammai is said to have allowed a proselyte, who was circumcised on the eve of Passover, to partake, after baptism, of the Passover, the school of Hillel forbade it. This controversy must be regarded as proving that at that time [previous to Christ] the baptism of proselytes was customary."[16] On the basis of this statement Doctor Strong holds that proselyte baptism was practiced at the time of Christ, and already before it.

John: That settles the matter. But what significance does this baptism have for the question of infants?

Martin: We shall soon see. The Gentile converts were, of course, adults. But if they had children and they wanted to take them with them into the covenant of God, they too were baptized. The Jews reasoned: Abraham was circumcised as an old man, Ishmael at the age of thirteen, and the infants at the age of eight days. The baptism of the proselytes was to follow the same pattern.

Gentiles abandoned the infants whom they did not want, and the Jews often took the foundlings into their care and baptized them. The boys were, naturally, also circumcised.

There was a tradition of the elders that a female proselyte was equal to native Jewish women in regard to marriage, if she had been baptized before she was three years and a day old. The rabbis explained: "If the profitableness of a thing is doubtful, it should not be done to a person who is not conscious of it. But it is permissible to do what is beneficial to a person who does not understand its value; and without his knowledge a person should not be harmed." Since baptism and acceptance into the covenant of God was beneficial, and leaving a child without it harmful, the rabbis declared infants had to be baptized.

In one respect proselyte baptism differed from circumcision: the proselytes' children who were born after their baptism were not baptized, because they were born "in holiness." [17]

Due to the strenuous missionary effort of the Jews, there were large numbers of proselytes both in Palestine and in the areas where the Jews lived in dispersion. Baptizing of families, parents with their children, infants and older, was therefore a common thing at the time of the public ministry of Christ. The Jews believed that the Gentiles were washed in baptism from the uncleanness of paganism, and that they were born again and became new men, children of the Covenant, and members of God's people, servants of the only true God. When John the Baptist called the Jews, too, to repent and be baptized, it must have seemed to them that they were placed on the same level with the Gentiles, and it was this that aroused the inquiry and criticism of the Sanhedrin, which sent messengers to John to ask him why he baptized. [18]

Now we have the necessary historical background for a proper understanding of the situation in which Christian baptism was instituted and first practiced. Families were taken into the covenant of God as units, parents with their infants and other children. Christ knew well the missionary practices of the Jews, and He criticized the Pharisees and scribes for making of their converts children of hell like themselves, [19] but he never criticized the baptism of infants. If He or the apostles had not approved it they certainly would have warned of it. Christ spoke of practically all the other errors and wrong practices of the Pharisees, but He never said a word about infant baptism. That cannot be merely accidental.

In this historical context we see in a new light the fact that the Apostolic Church also baptized whole families, like those of Cornelius, the Philippian jailer, and Stephanas in Corinth.[20] An unprejudiced mind would naturally suppose that the Church followed a practice similar to that customary among the Jews. The Church "inherited" many things—not only the Old Testament, but also many practices in its work and some features of organization—from the Synagogue. We know from the Acts that the life and work of the Apostolic Church took place within the framework of the Synagogue for a long time after Pentecost. Even after Paul had to leave the Synagogue in Greece and separate Christians from it about two decades after the birth of the Church, in Jerusalem and numerous other places the Synagogue continued to be the external framework of the Church. The Jewish Christians were very slow to realize all the implications of the New Covenant, and consequently continued to follow many of the Old Testament practices for a considerable length of time. A while ago we mentioned that they continued to use circumcision, although it was not in harmony with the plan and will of God. What could be more natural than that the early Christians, who continued to live within the framework of the Synagogue, following most of its practices, also followed its habit of baptizing the infants of converted parents. I repeat, Christ and the apostles never said a word against infant baptism, although it was commonly practiced by the Synagogue, and the Apostolic Church baptized families, just as the Synagogue did. Isn't it something entirely unnatural to think that Christ and the Apostolic Church would have rejected infant baptism, commonly used then, without saying a word on the matter? Isn't it much more reasonable to think that infant baptism is not mentioned because it was regarded as something so natural, so much a matter of course, that it did not need to be mentioned? When whole families were baptized, everybody understood that the Church followed at this point the ways of the Synagogue.

John: I have never looked at the question of infant baptism and the baptism of families from that point of view. You cannot, however, prove the existence of infants in those families. There are certain things from which we can conclude that there could not be babes in them. Paul preached the Gospel to the Philippian jailer's family before they were baptized, and they listened to his preaching and believed in God. Then they rejoiced in their new-found hope. How could such a record be made of unconscious infants? Those who were baptized were those who heard the Word, believed it, and rejoiced. In the case of Cornelius' family the same holds true, and of the family of Stephanas we read that they were the first fruits of Achaia, and addicted themselves to the ministry of the saints. This could not have been spoken of bap-tized infants, but well describes the Christian activities of adult believers.[21]

Martin: Let us assume that you have attended a service held by your pastor in a home which is made up of the parents and several children, the smallest of them a few weeks old and the oldest in their teens. You relate the event to one of your friends. Would you say:

"Our pastor held a service in the home of brother Frank Smith, preaching the Word to the whole family. They believed the Word and rejoiced over their faith in God."

Or would you put your story into a form like this:

"Our pastor held a service in the home of brother Frank Smith, preaching the Word to them, except to the infants and the small children, who, of course, could not understand it. They believed the Gospel and rejoiced over their faith in God, except the small children, who, of course, neither believed nor rejoiced."

John: I suppose the former way of telling about such an event is the common one, and I would use it unless I desired to be extremely cautious against the error of infant baptism.

Martin: Let us assume that a Baptist missionary comes from a certain district of India where he has opened a new mission field. He tells of a family which was first converted to Christianity and whose members became active laborers in the Lord's vineyard, being particularly willing to help and serve other Christians. Would he, in your opinion, put his story into the following form:

"The Pandita family was the first fruit of my work in India, except, of course, the little children, who did not understand and believe. They, namely the grown-up members of the family, dedi-cated themselves to the ministry of Christians there."

Or would he say:

"The Pandita family was the first fruit of my work in India, and its members dedicated themselves to the ministry of Chris-tians there."

John: Don't make fun of me. The latter form is, of course, the usual and natural form.

Martin: You defenders of the baptistic view yourselves make things funny and unnatural, when you think that the New Testament writers would have used such unnatural and artificial forms of speech in telling of the conversion and baptism of families. I do not assert that we can prove the existence of infants in the families mentioned in the New Testament. I only wanted to show that the nonexistence of little babes in them cannot be proved from the way the New Testament writers tell of them. But, as I said, since the baptism of families, infants included, was customary in the Synagogue, which was the external framework of the life of the Apostolic Church in most places, it seems quite probable that the principles of the Synagogue were followed, since the contrary is never stated. All the circumstantial evidence seems, anyway, to point in the direction of the use of infant baptism in the Apostolic Church.

John: I cannot deny that. However, mere circumstantial evidence is not enough to establish a Christian doctrine or practice.

Martin: You're right in saying that circumstantial evidence is not enough. It is, however, significant. You know how such evidence is sometimes of decisive significance, even in a court of justice. But let's turn to the express teachings of the New Testament. We may start with the Gospel record of children who were brought to Jesus to be blessed by Him.

3. Jesus and Children

John: That event cannot prove infant baptism, for none would have forbidden the parents from bringing their children to Jesus if He and His disciples had been in the habit of baptizing infants.[22] Besides, Christ did not baptize them. He only blessed them. We should do likewise.

Martin: Don't you think that the Lord's words show that His disciples held some erroneous views about children and their relation to Him?

John: Of course, they do, for the Lord rebuked them for their behavior. They did not do the right thing with regard to the children. The blessing of children should not be hindered.

Martin: Do you think that the disciples' error was due to the fact that Jesus was not in the habit of receiving children?

John: I stated a minute ago that none would have forbidden the parents from bringing their children to Jesus if He and His disciples had been in the habit of baptizing them. Maybe the reason was that Jesus had not been in the habit of receiving children.

Martin: Not at all. The narrative of Jesus and the children is in the nineteenth chapter of Matthew. In the previous chapter we are told that Jesus "called to him a little child, and set him in the midst of them, and said, Verily I say unto you, Except ye turn, and become as little children, ye shall in no wise enter into the kingdom of heaven!" [23] Doesn't this passage show that, shortly before, Jesus had shown His love for children and set them as examples of a right attitude for entering into the kingdom of God?

John: You are right there. I haven't noticed that this event had taken place before the children were brought to Jesus.

Martin: The first disciples were slow in understanding the Lord's will with regard to little children. Don't you think, brother John, that the disciples of our times may have a similar tendency to misunderstand His ways and thus fail to do what He wills?

John: We all understand only in part. The danger of misunderstanding the Lord's will is always present with us as long as we live in this world of imperfection. But as it seems to me, the misunderstanding in the case of little children is with you. We follow the example of Jesus and bless them, and there can be no misunderstanding about that.

Martin: That question is to be decided by a study of the teaching of Christ, of course. But I have a question for you: In the teaching and practice of your church, is the time of baptism the decisive thing, or the state of soul? In other words, is the decisive thing the age of the baptized person, or his faith?

John: The faith is, of course, the decisive thing, not the age.

Martin: Do you think that it is right to baptize believing children, or must they have reached a certain age?

John: I already said that the age is not decisive. The only limit is the ability to understand the Gospel and believe. We do baptize children who have a personal saving faith.

Martin: I have another question for you: How, or in what manner, do we receive the kingdom of God?

John: By faith, of course. The kingdom of God can be received by faith alone.

Martin: Do you, then, think that a person who receives the kingdom of God has a saving faith?

John: I do. Since the kingdom of God is received by faith, the person who receives it must be a believer. Since infants cannot believe, they cannot receive the kingdom of God.

Martin: Don't be too rash in your conclusions. Let's see what the text says. When the children were brought to Jesus He said of them, "of such is the kingdom of God." Then He went on to say, "Verily I say unto you, whosoever shall not receive the kingdom of God as a little child, he shall in no wise enter therein." Don't you think that, according to these words, the little children received the kingdom of God?

John: I don't think so. The Lord did not say that the little children received the kingdom, He only said that grown-up people must become as little children, small and humble, in order to receive the kingdom of God.

Martin: Let's assume that we are in a shipwreck near the shore and I tell someone: Unless you swim as John does, you cannot get to shore. Or I say: Unless you read and write as John does, you will not be accepted by the school. Do you think that John can be set as an example in something that he is not able to do?

John: Of course not. I was inconsiderate in my argument. But I have another one. Christ says, "Of such is the kingdom of God." He does not say that they receive the kingdom of God, but that the kingdom is theirs, that is, they already have it.

Martin: Now you are still more thoughtless from your own point of view. A short time ago you said that a person who has received the kingdom of God is a believer. Now you say that the little children already had the kingdom of God. Thus you hold that they were believers. And you also said that believing children should be baptized.

John: But maybe the words of Christ do not imply that the children already were believers, or that they believed on that occasion. The words may simply mean that these children had a relationship to the kingdom of God. What that relationship is, is taught elsewhere, namely, that they are under the care of believing parents and of the Church.

Martin: Is that what you read in the text? I do not read in it that the children only were in a relationship to the kingdom. The Lord says, "Whosoever shall not receive the kingdom as a little child." Little children do not have the kingdom just because they are little children, as some people think. Christ says expressly and emphatically, "That which is born of the flesh is flesh." [24] The kingdom of God belongs to little children in the sense that they are acceptable to it, and able to receive it when it is offered to them. They are welcome to Christ, as He says, "Suffer the little children to come unto me." When they come or are brought to Him, He gives them the Kingdom, and they receive it. They do it in faith, for that is the only way in which God's kingdom can be received.

A short while ago you admitted that believing children can and should be baptized. Since these children were believing children, wouldn't it have been right to baptize them?

John: I admit that they could have been baptized. But why weren't they baptized?

Martin: You already have admitted that it was not because they were children. Neither was it because they were unbelievers. I think the reason was that Christian baptism in its actual sense had not been instituted as yet, neither did the Christian Church in the full sense exist. True, John had been baptizing, but his baptism had not been a Christian baptism.

John: We believe that the baptism of John was essentially Christian baptism, although the full significance of it was not understood until after Jesus' death and resurrection.[25]

Martin: Do you, then, believe that the Christian baptism was actually instituted by John and not by Christ?

John: Not exactly that. But John's baptism was a baptism of faith in the coming Messiah, and it was a baptism of repentance for sin. The only difference between John's baptism and the baptism of our time is that John baptized upon profession of faith in a Savior yet to come, whereas baptism is now administered upon profession of faith in a Savior who has actually and already come.[26]

Martin: True, John pointed to Jesus and exhorted people to go to Him and believe in Him. But the question is: Does the New Testament teach that it was John who instituted the Christian baptism, with Jesus continuing it, or was it Jesus who instituted baptism, with John preparing the way for Him and for the baptism He instituted?

John: I think it is more correct to say that it was Jesus who instituted Christian baptism, and that John prepared the way.

Martin: John was Jesus' forerunner, and his baptism was the forerunner's baptism, a preparatory baptism, not the actual Christian baptism. We see it from Acts, chapters eighteen and nineteen. Appollos was an eloquent man and taught the ways of the Lord, but he knew "only the baptism of John." [27] The word shows that there was another baptism, distinct from the baptism of John, namely, the Christian baptism. While Appollos was in Corinth, Paul met in Ephesus twelve disciples who had been baptized with the baptism of John, and who knew nothing of the Holy Spirit. They were given instruction in the relationship between John and Christ, and then they were baptized with the Christian baptism. Doesn't that show that the baptism of John was not the same as Christian baptism? It was not sufficient in the Christian Church, but people who had received only the baptism of John were baptized with the Christian baptism when they accepted Christianity.

John: We believe that the baptism of the twelve disciples in Ephesus was not a new baptism but the baptism for the first time of certain persons who had been wrongly taught with regard to the nature of John the Baptist's doctrine, and so had ignorantly submitted to an outward rite which had in it no reference to Jesus Christ, and expressed no faith in Him as a Savior. This was not John's baptism, nor was it in any sense true baptism. For this reason Paul commanded them to be baptized in the name of the Lord Jesus.[28]

Martin: The twelve men whom Paul met in Ephesus were called disciples, a title used of Christians, and they associated with Christians. Your idea that the baptism they had received had had no reference to Christ has no basis in the text. The text tells only that they were ignorant of the Holy Spirit, not that they were ignorant of Jesus. Possibly they had lived at the time of the Pentecost in a region which had not been in contact with the events in Jerusalem.[29]

John: Maybe you are right. But what significance does this thing bear to our problem?

Martin: One more thing before we return to the question of why Jesus did not have the children baptized. Jesus made disciples to Himself, at least in the early part of His public ministry, by baptizing them through the agency of His disciples, as we read in the third and fourth chapters of John. Although this baptism belonged to the preparatory phase of Christianity, it seems to have been valid in the Church, for we have no record of those who were thus baptized to have been rebaptized. It was a baptism given at the command of Jesus, and people became His disciples through it.

John: Why, then, didn't Jesus have the children baptized when they were brought to Him?

Martin: The probable reason was threefold: first, the people Jesus called to be His disciples were to be the witnesses of His teaching, miracles, suffering, death, and resurrection. Little children were not fit for such a task. Second, when the children were brought to Jesus the Christian Church in the full sense did not exist. Believing children need Christian homes and a Christian Church. Jesus was on his way to Jerusalem, probably east of Jordan, for the children were brought to Him a short time before

His arrival at Jericho. In that region He probably had very few
disciples among the adult people. The Christian Church was
necessary before children could be baptized, for although acceptable to the kingdom, they needed the care of older Christians.
Third, since Jesus was on his last journey to Jerusalem, His suffering and death were only a few days away. We have no record of
baptisms of that time. Even those who had been baptized before
and were somewhat established in their discipleship could hardly
cope with what happened in Jerusalem. Baptizing started again
after the disciples had received the Holy Spirit, and the Christian
Church in its full sense was born.

John: Your explanation sounds plausible.

Martin: The fact that the children who were brought to Jesus
were not baptized is therefore no argument against the baptism
of believing children. Do you admit that?

John: I do. But all this has nothing to do with infant baptism.
The children who were brought to Jesus obviously were old
enough to understand the words of the Lord and believe in
Him. There is no objection to suffer them to come unto Him.
The question in the case of infant baptism is the bringing of infants to baptism who are too young to come by themselves. There
is no authority for such a thing.[30] We have no authority to call
tiny infants believers.

Martin: We are now coming to a crucial point, the age of the
children who were brought to Jesus. You assume that they were
at least four to ten years old. But our assumptions are not enough
here. We must have a definite text to base our opinion on. We
have such a text in the eighteenth chapter, fifteenth verse of Luke:
"And they brought unto him also their babes, that he should
touch them." In the original Greek text the word *brephos*
(plural *brephe*) is used here. This word has, according to Greek
lexicons, only two meanings: an unborn fetus, and a newly born
babe, an infant. Of course, only the second meaning is possible
here. Of these babes, or little children, as they also are called,
Jesus says, "Of such is the kingdom of God. Verily I say unto
you, Whosoever shall not receive the kingdom of God as a little
child, he shall in no wise enter therein."

Brother John, don't you see that your theory of the age of
these little children is not based on the Biblical text?

John: I must admit that. I have never investigated this text
that closely.

Martin: That's the very reason for many doctrinal errors; the
Scripture text is not studied closely enough. A short time ago

you agreed with me that the children who were brought to Jesus were believers, and that they could have been baptized if circumstances had permitted it. They were left without baptism because of some reasons of expediency, not because of principle.

John: Although I cannot find fault in your logic, I cannot believe that infants can have a saving faith. Faith comes by hearing. Infants cannot hear and understand the Gospel. It is against all sound reason, experience, and psychology to assume that infants can believe. Jesus did not say that these infants had faith. What He did say was that there comes a time when infants, no longer *brephe,* babes, believe, namely, when they have grown up and reached the age when faith is possible. Jesus did not even declare that the infants had received the kingdom of God.

Martin: Now you deny what you admitted before. Our text says that babes, *brephe,* were brought to Jesus. Later on they are called *paidia,* little children. You seem to think that the latter word refers to the later life of these babes. The text, however, contains no indication in that direction. The word *receive* is not in the future tense but in the aorist, which denotes a completed action at a definite point of time. I did not say that the infants had received the kingdom of God. The words of Christ show that they were able to receive it and did so when the kingdom was offered and given them. I am in complete agreement with you that the idea of infant faith is against all sound reason, experience, and psychology. My reason doesn't understand it at all and tends to be offended at such a thought. And as far as I am acquainted with psychology, the idea of infant faith is foolishness in the light of psychology.

John: Why do you, then, defend such a view?

Martin: What do you think, brother John: If there is a conflict between human reason, experience, and psychology on the one hand, and the plain teaching of Christ on the other, which of them should we accept as truth, if we are Christians?

John: The teaching of Christ is, of course, above all human reason, experience, and psychology. We do not want to be rationalists, who exalt their own reason above the word of God.

Martin: We have here a case in which Christ teaches one thing, and human reason, experience, and psychology teach an opposite thing. Christ says that infants, *brephe,* are acceptable to the kingdom of God—it is theirs. He also indicates that they receive it, since even grown-up people must receive it as infants. The reception can take place by faith only.

Human reason and psychology deny that infants can have

18

faith. Jesus says that they can. You have to choose, brother John, whether you follow your own reason and human psychology or Christ. I want to believe what Christ says of infants, even though I cannot understand it. Since the Lord says that infants can receive the kingdom of God, it is obvious that they also can be baptized, as you, too, actually have admitted.

John: I cannot deny that you reason logically from the literal sense of the words of Christ. In any case, it is plain that the proper subjects of baptism are those who give credible evidence that they have been regenerated by the Holy Spirit, or, in other words, have entered by faith into the communion of Christ's death and resurrection. Those only are to be baptized who have previously repented and believed. The Church is bound to demand of the candidate a reasonable proof of his repentance and faith. The believer's death and resurrection, set forth in baptism, implies, first, confession of sin and humiliation on account of it, as deserving death; second, declaration of Christ's death for sin, and of the believer's acceptance of Christ's substitutionary work; third, acknowledgment that the soul has become partaker of Christ's life, and now lives only in and for Him.[31] How can the infants fulfill these prerequisites of baptism?

Martin: They certainly cannot, if such conscious repentance and faith, and such confession of faith with the mouth, are required as its prerequisites.

But I have a question for you. Did Christ ask the infants who were brought to Him: Have you humbled yourselves to acknowledge your sinfulness? Are you ready to accept my substitutionary work and atonement? Do you profess faith in my deity? Can you give a credible proof that you have repented, have been converted, and have entered into the communion of my death and resurrection?

John: It is foolish even to ask such a thing. How could Jesus have presented such questions to little babes?

Martin: Naturally he did not. But don't you see that He simply received them as they were brought to Him, declaring with an emphatic divine assurance "Verily," that they were able to receive the kingdom of God, and that even older people had to become like them? You admitted that they could have been baptized if the circumstances had permitted it. Doesn't the example of Christ show what are the prerequisites of baptism in the case of infants? No questions concerning their repentance and faith should be presented to them. They should simply be received, through baptism, into the kingdom of God, the Christian Church, as Jesus received the infants.

John: He did not, however, baptize them, but only blessed them.

Martin: You return to that constantly repeated argument of those who oppose infant baptism. Have you forgotten how you already admitted that believing children can and should be baptized—and that the children who were brought to Jesus were left unbaptized because of expedience, not due to any principle?

John: I have no arguments left on that score. But I have another argument against infant baptism.

4. CHILDREN OF CHRISTIAN PARENTS

John (continues): Paul writes in First Corinthians, seventh chapter, fourteenth verse: "For the unbelieving husband is sanctified in the wife, and the unbelieving wife is sanctified in the brother: else were your children unclean; but now they are holy."

I think this text is a sure testimony against infant baptism, since Paul would certainly have referred to the baptism of children as a proof of their holiness, if infant baptism had been practiced. Moreover, this passage would in that case teach the baptism of the unconverted husband of a believing wife. It plainly proves that the children of Christian parents were not baptized, and had no closer connection with the Christian Church than the unbelieving partners of Christians.[32]

Martin: Both the opponents and defenders of infant baptism use this passage as an argument for their view. Let us examine what the apostle really means by it.

Paul teaches in this passage that if one parent, father or mother, is a believer, the rest of the family stands in a sanctified relationship, or lives in a Christian home, even though some member of it is an unbeliever. This sanctity of relationship, or membership in a Christian home, does not guarantee the salvation of the unbelieving partner or unbelieving children.

Doctor A. T. Robertson, a great Baptist New Testament scholar, says of the passage under discussion: "The verse throws no light on the question of infant baptism."[33] Thus a Baptist New Testament scholar refutes you in your use of this passage as an argument against infant baptism. What do you say to that?

John: Maybe Doctor Robertson is right. I withdraw my assertion that this passage can be used against infant baptism. But neither can it be used *for* it.

Martin: If you will bear with me, I will briefly explain the pedobaptist point of view with regard to this passage. We'll see then whether you accept or reject it.

Only the children of Christian parents were baptized in the Apostolic Church, for only they could have Christian rearing, living in the sanctified relationship of a Christian home. Paul says in the passage under discussion that the faith of one parent is sufficient to produce such a sanctified relationship. Thus even if only one of the parents was Christian, the children could be baptized.

Frequently it happened, of course, that the unbelieving parent did not want to have the children baptized. Thus in some cases the children were baptized and in others not, when only one of the parents was Christian. Since there was no general rule at this point, Paul could not say in this passage whether the children were baptized or not. He only said that the children lived in a sanctified relationship, in a Christian home, when one of their parents was Christian. As Charles H. Spurgeon says, such children "are favored by being placed under godly training, and under the hearing of the Gospel." [34]

Thus I do not say that infant baptism can be proved or disproved by First Corinthians, seventh chapter, fourteenth verse. But if it is proved otherwise, this passage fits well into the picture. Would you admit that much, John?

John: I think I would. When we are speaking of the relationship between Christian parents and their children, I have a question for you. Do you think that baptism belongs to the infant because of an organic connection of the child with the parents, which permits the latter to stand for the former and to make profession of faith for it—faith already existing genetically in the child by virtue of this organic union, and certain for the same reason to be developed as the child grows to maturity? I think some believers in infant baptism hold such a view. We object to it, for it unwarrantably confounds the personality of the child with that of the parent, and practically ignores the necessity of the Holy Spirit's regenerating influence in the case of children of Christian parents, and presumes in such children a gracious state which facts conclusively show not to exist. [35]

Martin: There may be some pedobaptists who hold such views as you mention. They cannot, however, be widespread, for I have never happened to meet people who have such views, neither have I found them in literature. There is, of course, a great amount of literature on baptism that I have never read, and therefore do not know what it contains.

As far as I am concerned, I think I have already made it clear that the sanctified relationship in which even the unbelieving members of Christian homes live is not based on any natural organic connection. It is a question of godly training and living in the sphere of the Gospel, as Spurgeon aptly says. Each person must have his own personal faith, which is always born by the regenerating influence of the Holy Spirit.

John: But doesn't Luther say that "infants are aided by others' faith, namely, of those who bring them to baptism"?[36] Luther seems to think that people who bring infants to baptism somehow, in a natural way, stand for them in baptism. However, believing parents obviously do not have an atom of merit for the salvation of their infants. Neither is there an atom of demerit in unbelieving parents that can condemn their infants, because Jesus is all in all.[37]

Martin: I am afraid you put your own ideas into the words of Luther. If you study his statement carefully you observe that he says nothing about the parents standing for their children or having any significance for their salvation because of their natural union with them. He only says that the child is *aided* by the faith of those who bring it to baptism. If you read the context of the words that you quoted, you see that Luther refers to the Gospel story of a man sick with palsy who was carried by his friends to Jesus. In a somewhat similar way the faith, prayers, and activity of believing parents help their children. Or don't you think that the faith of the parents helped the infants to come to Jesus in the case we have spoken of?

John: Of course it did.

Martin: I am afraid you were inconsiderate in speaking of the merit and demerit of parents for the salvation or perdition of their children. I suppose that you actually meant to say that the merit of believing parents cannot in any way substitute for the personal faith of the children, and that the demerit of the unbelieving parents cannot destroy the salvation of the children who believe in Christ. Don't you think that the prayers, tears, instructions, and entreaties of Christian fathers and mothers have any significance to the children from the point of view of their salvation? And that the ungodly life and bad example of unbelieving parents in any way promote the perdition of their children?[38]

John: There is no question of that. I fully realize the worth of

Christian rearing, as well as the dangers implied in the example of ungodly parents. My only objection is to the view that the faith of the parents would substitute for the faith of their children. But since we are unanimous on this point, let's pass to another question.

5. THE BAPTISM OF JESUS

John (continues): Jesus was baptized, as we know, when He was about thirty years old. Doesn't His example show that men should be baptized as adults?

Martin: Jesus was baptized by John. Do you know how much older John was than Jesus?

John: I think the difference in their ages was about six months, that is, they were of nearly the same age.

Martin: Do you know how old John was when he began to preach and baptize?

John: He was about thirty years old.

Martin: How could Jesus have been baptized when He was younger, since the baptism of John did not exist then? If the first pagan converts baptized by missionaries in a new field were about thirty years old, does that prove that they were never going to baptize infants? I think not. Missionaries who believe in infant baptism certainly will later baptize the infants of Christian parents.

John: But what was, then, the significance of the baptism of Jesus?

Martin: There are various opinions on the matter. Some commentators say that our Lord submitted to this ordinance in order to indicate His essential oneness with the human race, and thus identify Himself with sinners. Others say that it was primarily an act of humility, designed to be an example to us. Some folk seem to feel that our Lord submitted to this rite in order to indicate the proper mode of baptismal administration, that is, that it should be done by immersion.[89]

John: Isn't it true that the example of our Lord shows the proper mode of baptismal administration?

Martin: Maybe you are right. But let's postpone that question until the time when we shall discuss the mode of baptism.

I think you will have more respect for my explanation if I follow a Baptist author. In my view, Doctor A. F. Williams gives a good interpretation of the meaning of the baptism of Jesus, which is, in effect, that Jesus Himself gives us a key for the right understanding of the meaning of His baptism when He says, "Thus it becometh us to fulfill all righteousness." These words have been interpreted to mean, either that He was baptized to fulfill the righteousness required of *Him,* or that He intended to show *us* the importance of baptism if *we* would fulfill all righteousness. We find the right interpretation if we pay attention to what is the righteousness that God requires of us, and which Jesus came to fulfill.

God is holy and righteous, and before Him can stand no one who is sinful and unrighteous. But, according to the Scriptures, all men are sinful and unjust and deserve to be banished forever from the holy presence of God. But God in His mercy has provided for us the righteousness that His law requires, and He has done it through the death and resurrection of His Son. According to Paul, baptism means burial and resurrection with Christ.[40] Jesus spoke of His suffering, death, and resurrection as a baptism.[41] When He received baptism from John He indicated thereby that all righteousness was to be fulfilled and provided for men through His death and resurrection—although that could be understood only when these things had come to pass. Thus our Lord's baptism by John was a foreshadowing of His death and resurrection, through which He fulfilled for us sinners all righteousness and so made it possible for us to become righteous and well-pleasing in God's sight.[42]

John: That interpretation sounds very good. But doesn't the baptism of Jesus also mean that thereby He sanctified this rite for the use of His Church?

Martin: I believe it does. The interpretation that I just gave, following Doctor Williams, and the one mentioned by you do not exclude each other. But a special command from Christ was necessary for the institution of Christian baptism.

Since we have discussed the meaning of the baptism of Jesus, let us turn to the study of the significance of *our* baptism.

NOTES

I. Infant Baptism

1. Augustus Hopkins Strong, *Systematic Theology* (5th ed., revised and enlarged; New York: Armstrong and Son, 1896), p. 537.
2. The *Augsburg Confession* (VII) and *Smalcald Articles.* The Reformed Churches teach about the same. The *Belgian Confession* (XXVII) de-

fines the Church as "a holy congregation and assembly of true Christian believers."

3. Gal. 6:16. I Cor. 10:18.
4. Rom. 4:11.
5. Edward T. Hiscox, *The New Directory for Baptist Churches* (Philadelphia: American Baptist Publication Society, 1894), pp. 487f. In recent times a certain Baptist has said about the same thing: "There is absolutely no connection whatsoever between circumcision and baptism." (Quoted by J. Oliver Buswell, Jr., "Both sides of the Baptism Question," reprinted from *The Bible Today*, 1944-49, p. 14.)
6. Col. 2:11f.
7. Gen. 17:7.
8. Rom. 3:1-2.
9. Deut. 10:16.
10. Deut. 30:6.
11. Jer. 4:4; 6:10; 9:26.
12. Rom. 2:28, 29; 15:8. Phil. 3:3.
13. Rom. 3:3.
14. Matt. 23:15.
15. Strong, *op. cit.*, mentions such writers, p. 521. A. Wiberg declares in his book *Are You Baptised?* (originally published in Swedish, then in a Finnish translation, and possibly in other languages) that proselyte baptism was not used in the time of Christ. P. Lattu explains that the whole thing is uncertain in *Rajankäyntiä kastekysymyksessä Raamatun ja Historian valossa* (On the Problem of Baptism in the Light of the Bible and History), Helsinki, 1933, p. 30.
16. Alfred Edersheim, *The Life and Times of Jesus the Messiah* (New York: Longmans, Green and Co., Inc.), II, p. 747. Strong, *op. cit.*, p. 521.
17. Edersheim, *op. cit.*, pp. 746ff. Aapeli Saarisalo, *Messiaskuningas* (Messiah-King), (Porvoo, Finland, 1928), pp. 178ff. J. A. Maunu, *Kuvauksia Jeesuksen ajan historiasta* (Descriptions from the History of the Time of Jesus), (Porvoo-Helsinki, 1933), p. 250. Oscar Cullman, *Baptism in the New Testament*, (Chicago, 1950), pp. 26, 62.
18. John 1:25.
19. Matt. 23:15.
20. Acts 10:11; 16:33-34. I Cor. 1:16.
21. Hiscox, *op. cit.*, pp. 473-477.
22. Strong, *op. cit.*, p. 535.
23. Matt. 18:2-6.
24. John 3:6.
25. Strong, *op. cit.*, p. 521.
26. *Ibid.*
27. Acts 18:24-25.
28. Strong, *op. cit.*, p. 534.
29. Dr. H. A. Ironside, though an antipedobaptist, writes in his booklet *Baptism: What Saith the Scripture* (3d ed., 1930), pp. 12f., 17, that the

baptism of John "is quite distinct from Christian baptism." The testimony of John was but preparatory, and so was his baptism.

30. William L. Pettingill, "The Evils of Infant Baptism," in *The Voice,* official organ of the Independent Fundamental Churches of America, September, 1945, reprinted by Dr. J. Oliver Buswell, Jr., in *The Bible Today* (National Bible Institute, Shelton College, New York), and also in the booklet *Both Sides of the Baptism Question,* p. 2.

31. Strong, *op. cit.,* pp. 527ff. Similar statements in Hiscox, *op. cit.,* pp. 213f.

32. Strong, *op. cit.,* p. 535.

33. A. T. Robertson, *Word Pictures,* IV, p. 128. Quoted by Buswell, *op. cit.,* p. 44. We have, in part, followed Dr. Buswell in our interpretation of I Cor. 7:14.

34. Charles H. Spurgeon, *The Treasury of the New Testament,* I, p. 528. Quoted by Buswell, *ibid.*

35. Strong, *op. cit.,* p. 537.

36. Luther, *On the Babylonian Captivity,* Weimar ed., vol. 6, p. 538.

37. The thoughts in the last two sentences are those of a baptist, quoted by Dr. Buswell, *op. cit.,* p. 31.

38. We follow here, in the main, Dr. Buswell, *op. cit.,* p. 31.

39. When Hiscox deals with baptism of Jesus, *op. cit.,* pp. 398ff., the only thing to which he pays attention is the external mode of the baptism, saying not a word of its significance.

40. Rom. 6:4.

41. Luke 12:50.

42. Williams, "Christian Baptism as Set Forth in the Holy Scriptures." Published in Dr. Buswell's booklet *Both Sides of the Baptism Question,* pp. 19ff.

II. The Meaning and Blessing of Baptism

John: The churches that practice infant baptism seem to teach in general that salvation is conveyed through baptism. In my childhood and youth I was taught that baptism makes us children of God and heirs of eternal life, that it cleanses from sin, and works a new birth. All that is wholly unbiblical. The Scriptural doctrine is that a person must first be saved and then be baptized, for baptism does not save, neither has it power to cleanse from sin and work regeneration, to change the heart, or to sanctify the spirit.

Martin: Don't you believe that baptism has any saving significance to man?

John: Not in the sense that it would convey any grace. The doctrine of baptismal regeneration is an altogether false and pernicious doctrine. Regeneration is by the Holy Spirit alone and should precede baptism. Out of this mistaken view of the efficacy of baptism has grown the unscriptural dogma of infant baptism, since Christian parents in the third and fourth centuries had already begun to fear that dying infants could not be saved without it. Baptism is an outward sign of inward grace, showing forth the washing of regeneration and the renewing of the Holy Ghost that has taken place before. Baptism is not a means of grace. It is a confession of faith before men. It is not an act of God but a symbolical act of man, in which he obeys the command of Christ and confesses his previous regeneration and faith before men. Repentance, new birth, and salvation by faith in Christ are therefore prerequisites of baptism, not effects of it.

Since baptism symbolizes regeneration, it should be received after the new birth. It would be ridiculous to make the symbol precede the fact by many years.[1]

Martin: It is fine that you give such a thorough and plain description of the baptistic view of the meaning of baptism. Do you really believe that your doctrine is derived from the New Testament and based on its statements?

John: I do. Otherwise I would not hold it. The doctrine of a saving efficacy of baptism is a mere human tradition, and it is a pernicious tradition. The Bible never teaches such a doctrine.

26

1. SIGNIFICANCE OF BAPTISM ACCORDING TO THE SCRIPTURES

Martin: The matter is not decided if we merely declare that our doctrine is Scriptural. We must also show where the Bible teaches such a doctrine. Let's take our Bibles and study what the word of God says on these things. But before we start our study of the teaching of Scripture, I have a question for you. Do you really believe that infant baptism has grown from the idea of the saving and regenerating efficacy of baptism? Some time ago you admitted that infant baptism has grown from the words of Jesus concerning the infants; the kingdom of God is theirs, and they receive it. In our previous discussion we also arrived at the conclusion that the practice of the Synagogue has contributed to the use of infant baptism in the Apostolic Church.

John: I admit I was rash in saying that infant baptism has grown from the idea of the saving and regenerating efficacy of baptism. Nevertheless, I should not say that baptism has grown from the words of Jesus concerning infants. Rather I should say that the words of Jesus confirm the fact that the infants should be recognized as having a definite relationship under the care of the Church.

Martin: You repeat the argument that you gave before. I must also repeat mine: Jesus does not say that infants merely have a definite relationship under the care of the Church. He says that the kingdom of God is theirs, and that they receive it. You admitted that such children can and should be baptized. You also admitted that the use of infant baptism in the Synagogue has contributed to the practice of the early Church, since Jesus never opposed it, but by His words concerning infants indicated that they have the same position in the New Covenant as they had in the Old one. I do not, of course, oppose your statement that infants and children have a definite relationship under the care of the Church. I only hold that the New Testament teaches more than that.

John: At any rate, in practice, infant baptism and the idea of the saving and regenerating efficacy of baptism seem to go hand-in-hand.

Martin: We will soon study the question of the efficacy of baptism. But before that I wish to call your attention to the fact that there are people who oppose infant baptism and yet believe in the saving and regenerating efficacy of baptism. The Campbellites, also known as "Disciples," oppose infant baptism and use immersion. Nevertheless, they believe in a saving efficacy of baptism and in baptismal regeneration. If infant baptism would be a consequence of the idea of baptismal regeneration, why hasn't it had such a consequence in the case of the Campbellites?[2]

John: I admit that infant baptism and the idea of a saving and regenerating efficacy of baptism do not necessarily belong together. I retract my statement at this point. But I hold that what I otherwise said of the significance of baptism is Scriptural.

Martin: Well, let's see how the thing stands. Do you, brother John, believe that to become a disciple of Jesus is the same thing as entering into His kingdom?

John: I do. In the Apostolic Age, Christians were for many years simply called disciples. *Christian* was a name given them later in Antioch, as Luke tells in Acts, eleventh chapter, twenty-sixth verse.

Martin: Before His ascension Christ gave His disciples the command, "Go and make disciples of all nations, baptizing them . . . and teaching them to observe all things that I have commanded you." [3] Don't these words show that baptism and teaching are means that are used in making disciples?

John: Certainly not. Christ states there plainly that people must first be made His disciples and then be baptized and taught; first, the preaching of the Gospel and faith in it, through which people become Christ's disciples, and then baptism.

Martin: Faith in the Gospel is, of course, the main thing in becoming a disciple of Christ. Baptism and teaching would not make disciples, in the true sense of the word, without faith in the Gospel. In fact, a true living faith is the main thing in becoming a disciple. I don't think that we have any disagreement on that point. Still, what I said of baptism and teaching as means that are used in making disciples holds true. Let's imagine Christ giving a command like this: "Go and make disciples of all nations, preaching the Gospel to them, and teaching them to observe all things that I have commanded you." Wouldn't you understand in this case that the preaching of the Gospel and teaching are means used in making disciples?

John: Certainly. What other means could be used for that purpose?

Martin: Well, let's now compare the sentences: "Make disciples . . . baptizing them . . . and teaching them . . ." and "Make disciples . . . preaching to them . . . and teaching them . . ." Aren't these sentences grammatically alike?

John: They are; there's no question about that. But their meanings are not necessarily alike. All that the words of Christ prove is that baptizing is to go hand-in-hand with making disciples.

Martin: All right. Let's take them in that sense. Baptism must necessarily accompany the proclamation of the Gospel in making disciples. People cannot become disciples in the full sense without baptism. You probably know that the Jews and Moslems of our time do not regard a person as a Christian as long as he is not baptized, even if he believes in Christ. Until baptism he is in their eyes a Jew or Moslem. But from the moment he is baptized they regard him as a Christian. The same is true of the Christians. They, too, regard a person a true member of the Church only after baptism.

John: That's true, of course. But what is the significance of baptizing in the name of Christ, or in the name of the triune God? Doesn't it mean confession of His name before men?

Martin: I have a question for you. Who performs baptism in the name of the triune God? Who is the person who acts in it?

John: Naturally he who baptizes.

Martin: The person who is baptized only receives it. He does not primarily confess the name of the triune God, even when he is an adult person. He is baptized *into* the name of the triune God. The very act of baptism is therefore in conflict with your doctrine. Or do you otherwise confess the name of Christ before men while doing nothing but only receiving something from others, or being acted upon by them? Don't you confess Christ and your faith only when *you* do or speak something?

John: I hadn't thought of that. What you say is worth considering.

Martin: In First Corinthians, first chapter, second verse, Paul says that the Israelites were baptized into Moses in the cloud and the sea. Their baptism into Moses did not mean that they confessed Moses before men, but that they were put under the leadership of Moses, were dedicated to Moses, to obey and follow him as the God-ordained mediator and leader. The sea through which they traveled separated them forever from Egypt and from the rule of its king, and placed them under the government and leadership of Moses. In the same way we are separated from this world and its prince through baptism, being placed by it under the rule of Christ in His kingdom.

The same thing is seen from the question of Paul in First Corinthians, first chapter, thirteenth verse: "Were ye baptized into the name of Paul?" He does not mean: Did you confess the name of Paul in your baptism? but: Were you dedicated in baptism to Paul, to trust in him, to be under his rule, to follow him, and serve him? Weren't you baptized into Christ, to trust in Him, to be obedient to Him, and serve Him?

John: We also, naturally, believe that we dedicate ourselves in baptism to Christ, to trust in Him, and to follow Him.

Martin: Again you use the unbiblical baptistic language. Baptism is not your work, in which you act. You are acted upon in it. You are dedicated to Christ through baptism, and you dedicate yourself to Him through faith. Don't you see the difference? Baptism is an act of God and of His Church upon you. It must find a correspondence on your part by faith and surrender to Christ. Baptism is God's act upon you, faith and surrender is your act toward God. You have turned things upside down and made a human act of what in the Bible is an act of God. Isn't that a rather thorough perversion of an aspect of Christianity?

John: Don't be too hard on us. I will think of that. Maybe I have had a wrong idea of the meaning of baptism. But let's turn to another question. When Peter preached on Pentecost, there were about three thousand people who were touched, or pricked, in their hearts and asked what they should do.[4] Didn't they first hear and believe the Gospel and receive baptism after that?

Martin: A short while ago I told you that even those who practice infant baptism, that is, the baptism of the babes of Christian homes, first preach the Gospel to adult people and then baptize those who believe it. Baptism is a part of the Gospel. In it the Gospel promise is applied and "sealed" to individuals.

John: I do not agree with you in the view that baptism is a part of the Gospel. The risen Lord gives the commissions to His disciples in the closing chapters of the Synoptic Gospels. Luke does not mention baptism at all. He is occupied with the Gospel. Baptism is not a part of that, as Paul shows in First Corinthians, chapter fifteen, verses one to four, where he summarizes the contents of the Gospel and does not mention baptism at all, and as he indicates in First Corinthians, first chapter, seventeenth verse, where he says that Christ had not sent him to baptize but to preach the Gospel. The Gospel is concerning God's Son, as Paul says in Romans, first chapter, verses one to four, and not concerning ordinances, however blessed, or works, however proper,

Martin: Do you, brother John, really mean that Paul intends to the man already justified.[5]

to show the whole contents of the Gospel in First Corinthians, chapter fifteen, verses one to four, so that all things not mentioned in this passage but taught elsewhere in the New Testament are outside of the Gospel? For instance, Paul does not mention in that passage forgiveness of sins and justification by faith; neither does he mention Christ's dwelling in the hearts of believers, nor the parable of the lost sheep and the prodigal son. Do you think that all these teachings of the New Testament, and many others, do not belong to the Gospel?

John: I do not, of course, mean anything that foolish. At any rate, in First Corinthians, chapter one, verse seventeen, Paul makes a clear distinction between the Gospel and baptism.

Martin: In that passage Paul distinguishes the preaching of the Gospel and baptism, not the Gospel as such and baptism. On Pentecost, when people were pricked in their hearts and asked what they should do, Peter said that they should repent and be baptized in the name of Jesus Christ unto the remission of their sins. Do you think that these words of Peter no longer belonged to the Gospel? When a preacher shows what one should do to be saved, and how he can have his sins forgiven, is he no longer proclaiming and teaching the Gospel?

John: Of course, he is. I was rash in my statement. But baptism unto the forgiveness of sins means that this rite is a symbol of the forgiveness that people have first received, and an act of confession of the faith that previously has been born in them through the hearing of the Gospel.

Martin: Let's see what Peter actually said. "Be baptized unto, or into, the remission of your sins." "Into" is the literal translation of the Greek preposition *eis* that is used here. If you say that you dip your hand into water, do you mean that it is a symbolical act whereby you confess that you have previously immersed your hand into water? Don't you mean that the act of dipping takes your hand into water?

John: Your question is nonsense. Don't make fun of me.

Martin: It is you who make yourself ridiculous by saying that the phrase "to baptize into remission of sins" does not mean that baptism takes a person into the remission, or participation of the remission, but is an act whereby he confesses before men that he already has received the remission of sins. The people to whom Peter said these words were not yet partakers of the forgiveness of sins. They had not entered into remission of sins as yet. They were alarmed sinners who felt that they were sinful and condemned. They sought and asked for the remission of sins when they followed Peter's counsel and received baptism. It was baptism that took them into the remission of sins. Don't you see that this is the simple grammatical meaning of the words of Peter, and the meaning which also is required by the context?

John: I cannot deny that your explanation is in harmony with the grammatical meaning of the words. But how can an external rite convey the forgiveness of sins?

Martin: Christ said to His disciples that repentance and forgiveness of sins should be preached in His name.[6] Do you believe that the Gospel of forgiveness conveys remission to a penitent person who receives it in faith?

John: Of course, I do. How else could we have our sins forgiven except by faith in the Gospel, and in Christ on the basis of the Gospel?

Martin: The Gospel is an external thing. You hear it with your ears, or see it with your eyes. In baptism, the water, or the external rite, is connected with the word, and the word, or the Gospel, is the main thing in it. It is actually the Gospel that conveys the pardoning grace, and it is appropriated by faith. When the Bible says that a person is baptized into the forgiveness of sins, we accept this word and depend on this promise of the Gospel. Only by appropriating this promise of the word in faith do we receive the blessing of baptism. Don't you think that the word of God is worth believing?

John: I certainly do. I have never understood that you put the main emphasis on believing the word of the Gospel and not on the external rite. I have misunderstood your position on this point.

Martin: I'm glad our discussion helps us to understand each other better. Acts, second chapter, thirty-eighth verse, is not the only passage which speaks of forgiveness of sins through baptism. When Ananias came to Saul in Damascus, where he was praying with a penitent heart, he said to him, "Brother Saul . . . Arise, and be baptized, and wash away thy sins, calling on the name of the Lord." [7] These words show clearly that in baptism sins are washed away.

John: I believe the words "wash away thy sins" in this passage are metaphorical, just as the words "I am the vine, ye are the branches" are metaphorical.

Martin: Of course, they are metaphorical. Metaphor is a figure of speech in which one object is likened to another by speaking of it as if it were that other. The thing to which the word "wash" refers is removal of sin, or forgiveness of sins. Biblical metaphors refer in general to real things. In the statement that you quoted, our Lord likens the communion between Him and His disciples to the union between the vine and its branches. As the branches are dependent on the vine and receive their life from it, so are believers dependent on Christ and receive their life and power for fruitbearing from Him. In Acts, twenty-second chapter, sixteenth verse, the outward washing is a metaphor of the inward cleansing from sin, which takes place by the blood of Christ in and through the outward washing, by faith in the Gospel promise.

John: Baptism is an outward symbol or sign of inward grace, and in it a person gives testimony of the washing from sin that has taken place by the blood of Christ, through faith in the Gospel.

Martin: That's what you already said before. If your doctrinal formula is applied to the passage in Acts, Ananias intended to say to Saul: "Brother Saul . . . since you have already received the forgiveness of your sins in the blood of Christ, arise and be baptized as a symbol of this forgiveness and as a confession of your faith before men." But such a meaning of the words of Ananias is nonsense in this context. Saul was a penitent sinner when Ananias came to him. He knew that Christ was the Messiah and he called upon His name. But he received the remission of sins in baptism, and the Holy Spirit came upon him when Ananias laid his hands on him.[8]

John: I admit that you seem to be right with regard to the simple grammatical and historical meanings of the words. But isn't faith the prerequisite of baptism?

Martin: The New Testament teaches in the passages that we have studied only repentance as the prerequisite of baptism. Forgiveness is received *in* and *through* baptism, for the penitent sinner is baptized *into* the remission of sins. Or can you deny that this is the simple grammatical meaning of the words?

John: I cannot deny that. But baptism into the forgiveness of sins was for the Jews only. That nation had forfeited the favor of God, but those members who confessed their guilt and were baptized in the name of the Crucified One were manifestly snapping the link that bound them to the apostate people, and so they were out of the group on which the governmental wrath must fall. Their sins were remitted in baptism administratively. They would share in the judgment to come upon the Messiah-rejecting Judah. The administrative governmental forgiveness received in baptism referred to earth, not to heaven. It was concerned with God's dealings with the people of Israel in a governmental way. The governmental judgment was averted by baptism. The Gentiles are never told to be baptized for the remission of their sins. Paul was a Jew, and it was because of that that his sins were washed away in baptism, in a governmental sense. In baptism, he was transferred from the Jewish ground, and his sins were washed away in that sense. It was not a question of his eternal salvation. Of course, in a general sense, even among Gentiles one's sins can be said to be remitted by baptism—however, as also in John, twentieth chapter, twenty-third verse, not before God, but before the Church; that is, past sins are no longer held against the baptized person by the public body of believers.[9]

Martin: I am quite astonished at what you say. I was not aware that those who hold the baptistic view of baptism understood the relationship between baptism and forgiveness in that way. The views that you set forth probably are not generally held in baptistic circles, though held by some prominent teachers.[10] If you deny that baptism confers forgiveness, I guess the only way you can get by the passages that speak of baptism into the remission of sins is to limit them to the Jews, and to understand them in the governmental sense, as you call it. But when you do so you must answer the questions: Where does the New Testament speak of a "governmental forgiveness"? Where does it say that the significance of baptism is different for Jews and for Gentiles? Where does it teach two different kinds of forgiveness, one on earth and another before God? My New Testament teaches that there is no difference between the Jews and the Gentiles as far as salvation is concerned. Both are sinful and lost alike and are saved in the same manner. Baptism is a baptism into the forgiveness of sin to both, with no distinction between the two. Christ does not say in John, twentieth chapter, twenty-third verse, that when His disciples remit sins they are remitted only on earth and before the Church. He says "they are remitted unto them." And in Matthew, eighteenth chapter, eighteenth verse, the Lord says expressly, "Whatsoever ye shall loose on earth shall be loosed in heaven." Notice "in heaven," not on earth only. Where have you found in the New Testament your ideas of two different kinds of forgiveness—we are not speaking of reconciliation between men—and of a "governmental" or "administrative" forgiveness? Will you please show me the passages?

John: I cannot show any passage, but I deduce that doctrine from the fact that the Gospel had to be preached first to the Jews, who were under the governmental wrath of God. The second reason is that it is hard to see how sins can be remitted before God in baptism.

Martin: You, I mean those who hold the baptistic view, require that we should produce direct statements which show that infants should be baptized. You deny that inferences, conclusions and deductions from the Scriptural statements have any significance in this matter.[11] But you cannot yourself produce a single Biblical statement which says that infants should not be baptized. Your doctrine is based on certain deductions and conclusions, not on any direct statements of the Bible. Thus you use a double standard, one for yourself and another for others. In my view, that is not fair and honest. Likewise, your doctrine of governmental forgiveness is a "deduction" of yours, and is not found in the Bible. The fact that the Gospel was to be preached first to the Jews was simply a practical order. It had nothing to do with the manner or way of salvation. The New Testament speaks of one baptism only, and it is the same for the Jews and for the Gentiles. And there is only one forgiveness, that before God, which, however, is at the same time the forgiveness of the Church. This forgiveness takes man into the relationship of reconciliation to God, and into the membership of the Church.

As far as your second argument is concerned, namely, that it is hard for you to see how sins can be remitted before God in and through baptism, I am certain that we should simply believe what the word of God teaches. You have already admitted that in its literal sense it teaches forgiveness of sins in baptism.

John: I confess that I did not study carefully enough the idea of governmental forgiveness from the Bible. I accepted it too hastily from our teachers. I admit that this doctrine is not found in the Scriptures and I therefore give up the whole idea.

Martin: I appreciate your honesty and humble submission to the word of God. That shows that you have a Christian heart despite your erroneous doctrinal views. But in order to understand the teaching of the whole New Testament we should study other passages that speak of the saving efficacy of baptism. One of the most significant of them is Paul's statement in Ephesians: "Christ also loved the church, and gave himself for it; that he might sanctify it, having cleansed it by washing of water with the word," [12] or literally, "by means of (instrumental dative) the washing of water, in the word." [13]

The literal grammatical meaning of this statement is: The purpose of Christ's giving Himself to suffering and death is the sanctification of the Church. This sanctification takes place by means of the washing of water, in the word, or, if we take the Revised Version translation, after having washed it by means of the washing of the water in the word. Water is here the means used in washing or cleansing, but this washing of water is "in the word," that is, it is based on the word of God and connected with that word. This word is the commandment of Christ and His promise concerning baptism, given by Him and His apostles. It is proclaimed in connection with baptism and gives it its meaning, showing what it signifies and works. Washing with water is a metaphor of cleansing from sin, or blotting out of sin; but through the word it is at the same time a *means* of this cleansing.

Paul does not write: That he might sanctify it, first cleansing it by His blood, through the word, and then symbolizing it in the washing of baptism, in which the saved person publicly professes his faith before men. He simply says, "by means of the washing of water, in the word." Or can you, brother John, understand this passage in any other way, if you take it literally, in its grammatical sense?

John: Your explanation seems to be grammatically correct.

Martin: Let's turn to the first epistle of Peter. We read there: "The like figure whereunto even baptism doth also now save us (not the putting away of the filth of the flesh, but the answer of a good conscience toward God), by the resurrection of Jesus Christ." [14]

John: I understand those words of Peter as follows: Noah's salvation through the flood of wrath in the ark shadows forth the believer's deliverance from judgment, as baptism clearly expresses, that is, salvation by the work of Christ. He endured all the curse, even as the ark bore the brunt of the storm. The believer can say: His death was mine. It is not to baptism that the saving efficacy is attached. Baptism does not save. No rite saves. There is not the slightest justification here for the ritualistic dogma of baptismal regeneration. The only thing that gives the answer that the conscience demands is the resurrection of the Lord Jesus Christ from the dead. That apprehended baptism is full of meaning. [15]

Martin: I agree from my heart with much of what you say. Noah's salvation through the flood in the ark certainly foreshadowed the believer's deliverance from judgment by the work of Christ. However, I cannot agree with your statement that baptism does not save, and that no saving efficacy is attached to it. Peter says, "Baptism doeth save us." You say, "Baptism does not save." Don't you see that what you say is the direct opposite to what the word of God says? Nevertheless, you claim that your doctrine is Biblical. Is that honest? Isn't it poor interpretation to say that the word of God means the exact contrast of what it says? If the Bible does not mean what it says, but means something entirely different, how can we ever know what it means?

John: Don't be too hard on us. I cannot deny that in its literal grammatical sense this passage of Peter means that baptism saves. But how can it mean that? Isn't it true that only Jesus saves?

Martin: I certainly believe that only Jesus saves. We have no disagreement on that. Nevertheless, don't you think that when Jesus saves He can do it by using instruments, means, and agents, and save sinners through them? And if He uses means and agents, isn't it still He who saves? Let's assume that I fall from a ship and you throw me a rope; I take hold of it and you pull me up to the ship. Should I say "John saved me," or "The rope saved me"? I guess both statements could be true. The meaning would be: John saved me by means of the rope, using the rope as his instrument.

Likewise, Christ saves us, but He uses men as His agents for preaching the Gospel and performing the rite of baptism. He saves by using the word and the sacrament as His means or instruments. It is, however, He, He alone, who actually saves.

John: I have never considered the matter from that angle. I thought that baptism took the place of Christ. Now I see that when you speak of baptism as a means of grace you mean that it is an instrument that Christ uses. That makes a big difference.

But I have a remark to make on the words of Peter which we are discussing. I understand the words "putting away the filth of the flesh" to mean that it is not the external ceremony of washing, that is, the putting away of the filth of the flesh that saves. Salvation takes place through the inward cleansing by faith in which the conscience is purified by the resurrection of Christ. Baptism only symbolizes it. Hebrews, ninth chapter, thirteenth verse, speaks of Old Testament ceremonial cleansings to the cleanness of the flesh. I think Peter refers to such a cleansing here.

Martin: You're partly right and partly wrong. You are probably right in saying that the words "putting away the filth of the flesh" refer to the same thing as the verse in Hebrews. Peter says that baptism is not such a ceremonial washing as the Old Covenant washings were. He does not make any distinction between the external act and inward cleansing, as you do. He does not say: It is not the external washing that saves, but . . . He says that "baptism doth save us," not in the Old Covenant ceremonial way but in the New Covenant way. The Old Testament sacrifices and washings could not, as touching the conscience, make the worshipers perfect, as we read in Hebrews, ninth chapter, ninth verse. But the New Testament washing, baptism, does give a good conscience since the finished work of Christ, His resurrection, gives it its efficacy, while the Old Covenant washings were based only on typical sacrifices.

When Peter says that baptism is the answer of a good conscience toward God, he obviously means: When a penitent sinner goes to baptism he asks for the forgiveness of sins. In baptism he receives what he asks for. His sins are forgiven, and so he obtains a good conscience through the resurrection, or finished work, of Christ.

John: Your interpretation doesn't look bad. But Paul's words about being buried by baptism into death with Christ and of being raised with Him in Romans, sixth chapter, verses three and four, are not in harmony with your view. Burial and resurrection with Christ can come about only through faith. Baptism merely symbolizes this burial and resurrection, which has previoıﬂ occurred through repentance and faith. If the burial and resɐı rection with Christ cannot occur in an external ceremony, how can the cleansing of the conscience and obtaining a good conscience take place in it?

Martin: I am in complete agreement with you as far as the spiritual cleansing of the conscience and the spiritual buriᵃ resurrection with Christ are concerned. These things can take place only through repentance and faith. The appropriation of forgiveness and justification occurs through faith, and the nᴄw birth takes place by faith. But I do not see that there is any more conflict between baptism and faith than there is between the Gospel and faith. Through the Gospel and baptism the saving, pardoning, and regenerating grace is offered and given us, and we receive and appropriate it by faith. Baptism signifies and offers the grace of burial and resurrection with Christ, and faith accepts and uses it; or, in other words, in faith the burial and resurrection with Christ become an actual and living reality in our life; just as food is put into our mouth with a spoon, and we appropriate and use it by swallowing, digesting, and assimilating it. Or I may use an illustration that I employed a short time ago. I can say either that you saved me, or that the rope saved me, or that I was saved from drowning by taking hold of the rope and hanging on it. You are my actual savior, the rope is the means of my salvation, and taking hold of the rope and hanging on is my part in the matter. Likewise, Christ is the savior, the word and sacraments are the instruments, and faith is my taking hold of the promised grace, appropriating it, depending on it, and using it.

We were baptized into Christ's death and buried with Him through baptism. Baptism, connected with the Gospel, is a means whereby we are put into Christ's death, that is, placed under its shelter, so that it "covers" our sins. In baptism, we are made partakers of the blessings of Christ's death, burial, and resurrection as completely as if we ourselves had done all of it.

In ordinary speech, and according to ordinary grammar, the preposition "through" or "by" (in Greek *dia* with genitive) denotes means, instrument, way, channel, and so forth. The dictionaries explain that "through" means "by way of," "by means of," "by the instrumentality or aid of." The preposition "by" means "through the agency, means, or help of." You explain that these prepositions mean something like a symbol used afterward to show forth, exhibit, and confess what has happened before. According to ordinary grammar and common sense, these prepositions never have a meaning even remotely related to the sense you give it.

John: I cannot deny that you are right as far as the grammatical meaning of these words of Paul is concerned. I understand now your viewpoint in regard to this question better than I did before, and I admit that it does not look as bad as I had thought.

Martin: God's work in us has its external and internal side. The Holy Spirit uses in His work external means, the word and the sacraments, as well as agents, Christian people, ministers and others. I think that Luther is right when he explains that the Gospel is the actual and chief means of grace, from which the sacraments receive their efficacy. Even in the sacraments, grace is actually given through the Word, the promise of Gospel. Luther says in his *Small Catechism:* "It is not the water indeed that produces these effects, but the word of God, which accompanies and is connected with the water, and our faith which relies on the word of God connected with the water." Luther also says that the external element and the outward act of a sacrament are like a seal which confirms the promise of the Word in order to help us to believe it more firmly. As the document is the main thing and the seal only confirms it, so the Gospel word is the main means of grace; the sacrament is an external confirmation of the Gospel promise. Thus we can say that even in the sacraments grace is promised and imparted to us mainly through the word of the Gospel, with which is connected the sign or seal, that is, the element and sacred act.

The word that we hear with our ears and the sacramental act that we perceive with other senses are the external or instrumental side of the work of the Holy Spirit. Its internal and actual side is faith and the inward owning and experiencing of salvation. Without this inward side the word and the sacrament would not bring us any personal blessing, just as your throwing of the rope does not save me from drowning unless I take hold of it and hang on until I get back into the ship. Mere external hearing of the word and receiving a sacrament does not save unless the grace thus offered and conveyed is accepted in faith and becomes our own in the experience of salvation. Luther expresses this truth aptly: The Holy Spirit "teaches us to know the work of Christ and helps us to accept it and use it for our benefit . . . He does it externally and internally: internally through faith and spiritual gifts; externally by means of the Gospel, baptism, and the sacrament of the altar . . . through which He comes to us and renders the sufferings of Christ effective in us for our salvation." [16]

John: That explanation sounds pretty good. I had a suspicion that you harbored some kind of magical view of the efficacy of the means of grace. Now I see that you believe, as we do, that the inward work of the Holy Spirit is the actual and main thing, and the means of grace are only external instruments used by Him. I have nothing against such a view.

You hold that repentance, not a saving or regenerate faith, is the prerequisite of baptism in the case of adult people. There is, however, in the New Testament a passage which teaches that a person must have a saving faith before he is baptized. You remember the story of the Ethiopian eunuch in Acts eight. Philip proclaimed the Gospel to him, and he believed it. As the first act of the obedience of faith, he asked for baptism when they came to a place where there was water. Before fulfilling his request Philip said to him, "If thou believest with all thine heart, thou mayest. And he answered and said, I believe that Jesus Christ is the Son of God." [17]

Doesn't this passage show that a saving faith and regeneration were prerequisites of baptism?

Martin: The eunuch had a desire to be saved, and when Philip spoke to him of the necessity of repentance and of baptism into the remission of sins in Jesus' name, he naturally wanted to be baptized in order to have his sins forgiven and become a partaker of salvation. Such a person can sincerely answer that he believes Jesus Christ to be the Son of God. Philip did not ask him: Do you have a personal saving faith? Have you experienced the new birth so that you can give witness of it in baptism? Neither did the eunuch confess any experiences of his own, but only that he believed Jesus Christ to be the Son of God. The eunuch obviously had before baptism only a repenting faith, which became a regenerate faith in baptism, and so he "went his way rejoicing." You cannot prove from the text that regeneration was the prerequisite of baptism in this case.

John: At any rate, a saving faith is taught as the prerequisite of baptism in the words of Christ, "He that believeth and is baptized shall be saved; but he that believeth not shall be condemned." [18] Christ says here that one must first believe and then be baptized. He must first be saved and then confess his faith in the symbolical act of baptism.

Martin: In this passage our Lord says, "He that believeth and is baptized . . ." [19] The three thousand people on Pentecost believed the words of Peter, were "pricked" in their hearts and asked what they should do. They were called to repent and be baptized. The Ethiopian eunuch believed the Gospel before he was baptized. But in both cases the faith that was the prerequisite of baptism was a repenting faith that prayed and sought for salvation. That's what Christ also means in Mark, sixteenth chapter, sixteenth verse. The Lord does not say: He that believeth and is saved, shall be baptized, but "He that believeth and is baptized, shall be saved." Salvation is mentioned after baptism, not after faith, for it is given in baptism, even as Peter says, "Baptism doth also now save us"; namely, if we believe the Gospel. Thus this statement of Christ does not contain your doctrine at all, but is in a clear conflict with it.

John: What is, then, the meaning of the words that follow: "He that believeth not shall be condemned"? Don't these words mean that salvation does not depend on baptism but on faith? If baptism is a means of grace, then all the baptized should be saved.

Martin: Not at all. The Gospel is the chief means of grace, the power of God unto salvation, but it is such only to those who believe. Many people hear the Gospel but do not believe. Likewise, there are people who are baptized but are not saved because they do not believe. You remember Simon Magus in Samaria. He assumed that he believed, being amazed at the miracles done through Philip. But soon it became clear that his heart was not right before God. He did not have a saving faith, and consequently he was condemned, although he had received baptism. A means of grace imparts salvation, but it must be received by faith. An unbeliever is not benefited by it because he does not receive the gift offered in it.

John: You may be right as far as the meaning of the words in Mark are concerned. Still I hold that baptism is connected with the sphere of profession. We see that from the words of Paul in Galatians, third chapter, twenty-seventh verse: "For as many of you as have been baptized into Christ have put on Christ." This can only be true of professed believers, who, in this act, publicly put on Christ, or, in other words, acknowlege Him as their Lord. In the sixth chapter of Romans, Paul says, "Know ye not (R.V.: "Are ye ignorant") that all we who were baptized into Christ Jesus were baptized into his death." The words "Know ye not" cannot appeal to infants or persons incapable of understanding the truth of the Gospel. Likewise, when Paul says in the same chapter that the baptized should "walk in the newness of life," he cannot mean infants who cannot walk. Persons unable to walk are never contemplated as having been baptized at all.[20]

Martin: You understand that "to put on Christ" means to acknowledge or profess Him publicly as one's Lord. I have not found such an interpretation in the Bible. True, many people think that the main purpose of putting on clothes is to show them to other people. For me, the main purpose of clothing is to keep me warm and to serve as covering, because it is shameful to appear naked among people. Likewise, to put on Christ is to have Him as the covering of our sin-nakedness, as He Himself refers in Revelation, second chapter, eighteenth verse, and to be under His shelter and grace, so that He covers and surrounds us with His righteousness, grace and protection. In baptism we put on Christ in the sense that He covers us with His grace and righteousness. Each baptized person must appropriate and own all this by a conscious faith. An infant can well be clothed by the mother. It can be wrapped in clothes and be under the care of the mother, although it is little conscious of it. Likewise, an infant can be under the shelter and care of the Lord, surrounded by His forgiving love and righteousness, although it is not conscious of it. The sacred writers of the Bible sometimes speak of God's loving care of their life from their birth on, yea, from the womb of their mother. I do not see why it should be difficult for us to believe that in baptism an infant is received by

Christ to be in a special way under His care and "clothed" in His righteousness. The idea of putting on Christ by a public profession is your own. I do not find it in the Bible.

The words "Know ye not," and "walk in the newness of life" were written to Roman Christians after their baptism, in most cases a number of years after it. Paul naturally wrote primarily to adult Christians who needed to be reminded of what had taken place in their baptism. Those who were baptized as infants but had grown up and reached the age of discretion likewise needed to be reminded of what their baptism meant to them, and what obligations followed from it. The words of Paul apply well to a congregation of whose members some had been baptized as adults and others as infants or children. I do not see how these words can be used as a proof against infant baptism. You have already admitted that, according to the plain words of Christ, infants receive the kingdom of God. I believe that to receive the kingdom of God implies putting on Christ.

John: I cannot show any Scriptural passage that opposes your explanation. At any rate, faith alone gives value to baptism. Apart from faith it is a meaningless form, and therefore I think that a person should first be converted and then be baptized.[21]

Martin: You speak in that manner because you think that baptism is given on the confession of faith, and is itself a part of that confession, or profession. When the significance of baptism is understood in that way faith naturally gives value to it. But the matter is different when we take baptism in its Biblical meaning. According to the New Testament, a person is baptized into the death of Christ and into the forgiveness of sins, he puts on Christ, water saves him as baptism and so on. In a word, the Bible teaches baptism as a divine act on man and as a gift to him. These blessings have their value in themselves, whether they are received or not. If I give you a precious diamond, this diamond has its own value whether you receive it or not. But it has value *to you* only if you accept it, appreciate it, and use it. Likewise, baptism has its own value independently of faith, but the baptized person owns and enjoys its value for his personal benefit only by faith. True, it is a meaningless rite to the unbeliever, and he has no benefit from it, but in itself it is, nevertheless, a precious thing.

John: I was rash in saying that faith alone gives value to baptism. As a divine ordinance it naturally has its value in itself, when it is given in the Christ-ordained manner. But it has a real personal significance only to the believer.

Martin: Fine. We have a rather close agreement on this point. After all, our view in this respect depends on our understanding of the significance of baptism.

John: When considering the significance of baptism, I have a question for you: What is your conception of the relationship between baptism and regeneration?

2. BAPTISM AND REGENERATION

Martin: Christ said to Nicodemus: "Except a man be born of water and the Spirit, he cannot enter into the kingdom of God." Do you understand that the word "water" in this statement refers to baptism?

John: No, I believe the word "water" means here the word. The word is likened to water from its cleansing efficacy, and because it is by the word that the new birth is brought about, as James and Peter write.[22] This word is applied by the Spirit, and the believing sinner is born anew. The word "water" cannot here mean baptism, for Christian baptism was not instituted until after the Lord's resurrection, and it signified burial with Him unto death. Obviously that could not be the meaning nor effect till the Lord died. Christ spoke to Nicodemus of the regenerating work of the Spirit through the word, not the rite of baptism.[23] There are some people among us who think that the water means here the Spirit, for the Bible often speaks of the Spirit as the water of life. But I do not think that view is correct, for then we should change the text to run like this: Except a man be born of water, even the Spirit, he cannot enter into the kingdom of God. Those who hold this interpretation assert that the Greek word for "and" may be translated as "even."

Martin: I agree with you when you say that the word of God has a cleansing efficacy. Christ says, "Already are ye clean for the sake of the word which I have spoken unto you."[24] You also are right in saying that the new birth is brought about by the word, which is applied by the Spirit. But in this case the meaning of the word "water" is to be determined from its context. The Scriptures speak both of baptismal water and of the water of life. Let's turn to the Bible to find out what is the meaning of the word "water" in this context. When you read the third chapter of the Gospel of John, what is the water that it speaks of, the baptismal water or water in the figurative sense?

John: I see that it speaks of baptism, reporting that both John and Jesus baptized in the land of Judaea, though John remarks at the beginning of the fourth chapter that "Jesus himself baptized not, but his disciples."

Martin: You admit, then, that the context, the same chapter, speaks of the baptismal water. Jesus' words to Nicodemus must be understood in the context of the historical situation in which they were spoken. All Judaea and Jerusalem were aroused and agitated by the preaching and baptism of John. The big question in the minds of people was: Should we go to be baptized in water by John, confessing our sins? And soon they had a similar question concerning the baptism given by Jesus through His disciples. Nicodemus belonged to the Pharisees, of whom Luke tells that they did not humble themselves to repent and to receive baptism in water for the forgiveness of their sins.[25] When Jesus mentioned water to him, in that situation he could think of nothing other than baptism. The term "new birth" was commonly used among the Jews in connection with the proselyte baptism. Nicodemus was therefore well acquainted with the phrase "to be born of water." Your argument that Christian baptism was not instituted until after the Lord's resurrection has no force here, since baptism of repentance unto the remission of sins was practiced at the very time that Nicodemus came to Jesus. This baptism was at that time necessary for those who wanted to be prepared to receive the Messiah.

John: I withdraw my argument and admit that Jesus probably meant baptism in speaking of being born of water. But He also spoke of being born of the Spirit. The two belong together, and cannot be given to infants, who do not understand the word and believe.

Martin: Again you forget what you have admitted before, namely, that our Lord teaches infant faith when He says that they receive the kingdom of God. But you are right in saying that the birth of water and of the Spirit belong together. These two constitute the new birth. I have, however, a question for you: Do you think that Paul refers to baptism when he speaks of the "washing of regeneration" in Titus, third chapter, fifth verse?

John: It is quite usual among us to speak of baptism as a symbol of regeneration. If baptism symbolizes anything, it symbolizes regeneration.[26] In speaking in this manner we naturally have in mind the words of Paul in the passage in Titus.

Martin: Someone has recently remarked that there are different views of the meaning of the word "regeneration," or new birth.

Before we go on to discuss the relationship between baptism and regeneration we should agree on the meaning of the term new birth.

In the natural birth we become members of the sinful human race. In the new birth we become children of God and members of His people. The new birth implies a twofold change: a change in our relation to God and status before Him, and a change in our inward condition, mind and heart. In other words, regeneration implies a twofold saving gift: adoption or reception into the status of a child of God; and renewal of the heart, or creation of the mind and heart, of a child of God. The former takes place in forgiveness and justification, the latter in renewal by the Holy Spirit. The new birth occurs when a person receives Christ as his Savior. "As many as received him, to them he gave right (and power) to become children of God." [27] The Greek word *exousia* used here means both right and power, or, in other words, the status and mind of a child of God.

Do you, brother John, feel that this definition of the new birth is Biblical?

John: I do. I have nothing against it.

Martin: The "washing of regeneration" of which Paul speaks in Titus is the "washing from sin," or forgiveness of sins, that takes place in regeneration. Actually it takes place by the blood of Christ, for only Christ's redemptive blood can wash away sin. But this blood can be applied to a person, or his sins can be declared forgiven, either by baptism, connected with the word, or by the word alone. This application ordinarily takes place the first time in baptism. If a baptized person has fallen from grace and returns to it in repentance, it is applied to him by the word alone; he hears the assurance of forgiveness and cleansing in Christ's blood in the word of the Gospel. When Paul speaks of the washing of regeneration he probably means both the washing that takes place by *baptism and the word,* and the washing that occurs by the *word alone,* through faith. His primary reference, however, must be to the washing of regeneration in baptism. You remember how Paul himself experienced this very thing when Ananias baptized him, and his sins were washed away in it. The words of Christ of the "birth of water" refer to the same thing: washing from sin by forgiveness takes place in baptism "into the forgiveness of sins." The birth of the Spirit is the renewal of the heart from unbelief to faith and from disobedience to obedience. The Holy Spirit works when He comes into the heart.

These two gifts make up the new birth. But when God saves

men He does not always give the whole salvation in one bunch. We see this from several statements of the New Testament and from the life histories of a number of people of whom we have a record in it. Apostle Paul writes to the Galatians: "God sent forth his Son . . . that he might redeem them which were under the law, that we might receive the adoption of sons. And because ye are sons, God sent forth the Spirit of his Son into our hearts, crying, Abba, Father." [28]

Through the redemptive work of Christ we receive the adoption of sons. To those who have received this gift God sends His Spirit to bear witness with their hearts of this sonship and to cry "Abba, Father." Adoption is first, the Spirit after it, like the washing of regeneration is first, and the renewing of the Spirit after it.

John: Isn't that merely a logical order, not an order in time?

Martin: In a certain sense it is a logical order, and frequently it is only that. But there are several cases recorded in the New Testament in which it is not only a logical order but also a temporal order.

The first case is that of the first disciples. The Lord told them during His public ministry, before they received the Holy Spirit: "Already are ye clean because of the word which I have spoken unto you." [29] "Ye are clean." [30]

In the same night, Christ spoke of a cleansing bath: "He that is bathed needeth not save to wash his feet, but is clean every whit: and ye are clean, but not all. For he knew him that should betray him."

The disciples had received a cleansing bath through the Word and baptism by which they had become His disciples. Through them they had received an assurance of the forgiveness of their sins. They had this gift before Pentecost, or before the baptism of the Spirit. The Spirit had, of course, started His work in their hearts, so that they trusted in Jesus and wanted to follow Him. They were, however, rather carnally minded, and the actual renewal of the Spirit and enduement with power did not occur until Pentecost.

We have, in addition, three cases recorded in the Acts in which the work of God in men had two phases. When Philip preached the Gospel in Samaria, the people in that city "gave heed with one accord unto the things that were spoken by Philip." They were baptized, but did not receive the Holy Spirit then. "For as yet he was fallen upon none of them: only they had been baptized into the name of the Lord Jesus." When the apostles in

Jerusalem heard of the events in Samaria, Peter and John went there, prayed for the Samaritan converts, and laid their hands on them, and they received the Holy Spirit.[31]

There are people who interpret this passage to mean that the Samaritans actually received the Spirit in baptism, but were given the gift of tongues and some other gifts of grace through the laying on of the hands. This interpretation is, however, in plain conflict with the words of the text, and it is better that we let the text be as it is.

When Peter preached to the household of Cornelius, the Holy Spirit came upon the hearers when Peter said the words: "Through his name every one that believeth on him shall receive remission of sins." Peter and those with him were amazed, not only because the Spirit was bestowed upon Gentiles, but also because this gift was given before baptism. Peter commanded them to be baptized in the name of Jesus Christ.[82] In this case the gift of the Holy Spirit was received before baptism with water.

The third case is recorded in Acts, nineteenth chapter, verses one to seven. Paul found in Ephesus some disciples of John, and asked them: "Did ye receive the Holy Ghost when ye believed?" They said that they knew nothing of the Holy Spirit, probably meaning that they had no knowledge of the pouring of the Spirit upon disciples and no personal experience of it. They were then baptized in the name of Jesus, and when Paul laid his hands on them, they received the Holy Spirit.

In this case the Holy Spirit was received a short time after baptism, through the laying on of the hands. Paul's question, "Did ye receive the Holy Ghost when ye believed," indicates that a person can believe in Christ, in a certain sense, as the disciples believed before Pentecost, and as the Samaritans believed before Peter and Paul laid their hands on them, without then receiving the Holy Spirit.

John: Is it, then, a general rule that there are two phases in this work of God, or two stages on the way to a living faith?

Martin: No, certainly not. There were obviously numerous people in the Apostolic Age who came to faith and received the Holy Spirit, or were baptized with water and the Spirit, about the same time. But there were other cases in which the "coming to faith," possibly connected with baptism, was only a preparatory phase. These people *became full New Covenant believers* later, when they received the baptism of the Holy Spirit. God leads each person in the way He sees fit, and we should not prescribe any formula in this respect, as sometimes has been done. But the words of Paul to the twelve disciples in Ephesus, as well as the conduct of Peter and Paul in Samaria, however, show that *the Apostolic Church regarded it as very important and essential that people were not left on the preparatory stage but became partakers of the Holy Spirit and so had a living faith and power from on high.*

A peculiar fact is that *the New Testament contains no record of people receiving the Spirit at the moment of baptism.* That may, of course, have occurred, although no such case is recorded. Therefore those who hold that the Holy Spirit is always, or ordinarily, received in baptism have no sure foundation for their faith.

John: Do you think that people who are under the influence of Christianity and follow it to a certain extent are saved and inherit eternal life?

Martin: Christ is the final Judge of the living and the dead, not we. Among those who inherit the eternal kingdom there will probably be many people whom we have not expected to be saved; and there will be among the lost many whom we have regarded as true Christians. However, we all have full reason to take heed of the warnings of Christ lest we deceive ourselves. You remember His words at the end of the Sermon on the Mount:

"Not every one that saith unto me, Lord, Lord, shall enter into the kingdom of heaven; but he that doeth the will of my Father which is in heaven. Many will say to me in that day, Lord, Lord, did we not prophesy by thy name, and by thy name cast out devils, and by thy name do many mighty works? And then will I profess unto them, I never knew you: depart from me, ye that work iniquity." [33]

These words of Christ show that a person may assume, and even be quite sure, that he is a Christian. He has received baptism—either as an infant or adult—been a church member, made a Christian profession, attended church services and the Lord's Table, and even preached and taught others, and accomplished great things; yet he has never been really born of the Spirit. "If any man hath not the Spirit of Christ, he is none of his," Paul says.[34] If a person has not done the will of the heavenly Father, having repented of his sins, having been cleansed from iniquity by the blood of Christ, and renewed by the Holy Spirit to faith and obedience, he is not known by Christ and will be eternally condemned.

In His parable of the virgins, Christ tells that there were ten virgins who went to meet the bridegroom, but only five who were admitted to the marriage feast. The rest did not have oil in their lamps. They were therefore left without, for Christ did not know them as His own.[85] These foolish virgins are a picture of those church members who profess Christianity and have the form of godliness but lack its power.[86] They have all the externals —the lamp—of Christianity, but they do not have the saving grace and Spirit of God in their hearts; they lack oil in their vessels. I am afraid that great numbers of those who have been baptized as infants and rely on their baptism in a wrong way, without having a living faith, belong to the "foolish virgins." They will sometime have the horrible experience that Christ does not know them and will not admit them to heaven. There will also be, I am sure, great numbers of such people among those who have received baptism upon the profession of faith. Many people will say that they have heard the word of Christ and, as church members, received the sacrament of the Lord's Supper, assuming that they are Christians by that. But when Christ comes they will be left outside. The Lord will say to them, "I tell you, I know not whence ye are; depart from me, all ye workers of iniquity." Despite their baptism and active membership in the church, they have never really entered in by the strait gate.[37] They have never truly been born of the Word and Spirit of God. They have never been Christ's own, His sheep, who hear His voice and follow Him.[38]

These are solemn warnings from Christ lest any man deceive himself. The Gospel and the sacraments are blessed things, but we are saved only if, through them, we are truly born of the Spirit, hear the voices of Christ, follow Him and do the will of the heavenly Father. True repentance and faith in Christ are necessary, whether baptism is received in infancy or later.

John: I agree with you. I know that there are many people who are baptized upon the profession of faith but are not truly born of the Spirit. Christ's parable of the sower applies here. There are people whose hearts are like the rocky places of this parable; they receive the Word with joy and profess faith, but it is all shallow and superficial. Their heart has remained unchanged, and so they soon fall away. Others are like those in whom the Word is sown among the thorns; it first begins to grow, and they profess faith for a while, but the roots of the thorns have remained in their hearts all the time, and soon they choke the Word. We all have reason to examine ourselves lest our profession of Christianity be superficial and untrue.

Let's turn back to the question of the relationship between baptism and regeneration. I admit that the New Testament speaks of a birth of water, or new birth of the water and the Spirit. But in most cases it teaches regeneration through the word of God. The Christians have been born (begotten) again of the incorruptible seed of the word of God.[39] God has begotten them by the word of truth,[40] or through the Gospel.[41] The Bible also says that the Christians are born of God, or of the Spirit.[42] The meaning seems to be that God, or the Spirit, works the new birth, using the word of the Gospel as His means and Christians as His agents. How do you fit together the passages that speak of regeneration through the Word and the ones that speak of it through baptism?

Martin: I am glad that you've brought up that question. The fact that the New Testament in most cases speaks of the new birth through the Word shows that those people cannot be right who hold that regeneration always and without exception takes place through baptism and baptism alone.

The Word, the Gospel, is the chief means of grace. Even in baptism the Word is the main thing. The sacramental rite only "seals" the promise of the Gospel to the baptized person individually. I think I do not need to dwell on this point any more.

In the *spiritual sense* the new birth is the same as the *kindling of a living faith* in man's heart. Faith does not only imply trust in Christ as a personal Savior and dependence on Him for forgiveness and justification; it also means an experiential knowledge of Christ, communion with Him, love for Him, surrender to His teaching and rule in willing obedience and, as its fruit, confession of His name among fellow men by word of mouth and a holy walk in love and truth. The Holy Spirit works all these things primarily through the Word. As compared to the Word, the sacraments are of secondary value, being in the service of the Gospel word. Therefore Paul writes that Christ had not sent him to baptize but to preach the Gospel.[43]

Baptism is, of course, a part of the Gospel, being in its service as an external means for applying and "sealing" it to man personally. We may also say that in it the rays of the Gospel are focused on one person. Still, it is the Gospel which is the power of God unto salvation to everyone who believes.[44] The saving efficacy of baptism is the saving efficacy of the Gospel, since it is a servant of the Gospel and a special mode of the Gospel application.

John: Now I see the matter more clearly than before. According to your conception, baptism is a form of Gospel application and as such a *work of God to man,* in order to help him to become a partaker of salvation in Christ. According to the baptistic view, baptism is a fruit of faith, *man's work toward God and his fellow men*, to whom he confesses his faith by accepting baptism. The baptistic baptism seems to be, as to its meaning and content, an entirely different rite from yours. However, it seems to me that what Paul says of circumcision in the case of Abraham applies to the baptistic understanding of baptism: Abraham received circumcision as a seal of the righteousness that he had before it. Likewise, the baptistic view regards baptism as a seal of the righteousness and salvation that they have before it. Doesn't this conception apply to cases in which, as in that of Cornelius, the saving faith and Holy Spirit are received before baptism?

Martin: I think you're right as far as instances like Cornelius' are concerned. In such cases, baptism is a seal of the salvation which such people already have received. But those who have the baptistic conception do not in general speak of baptism as a seal. They speak of it as a symbol which is used in confessing faith and salvation. Baptism as a seal is God's work on man, whereas baptism as a symbolic act of confession is man's act. Thus the words of Paul concerning Abraham do not apply to the baptistic view. Besides, you holders of the baptistic view generally deny any connection, or even analogy, between circumcision and baptism. To be consistent, you should not do it here, either.

I hope you see now that the baptistic view and the pedobaptist understanding of baptism are so different and contradictory that they cannot be harmonized in any way. One of them must be Biblical and the other entirely unbiblical. I do not find a trace of the baptistic doctrine of baptism in the Scriptures, as far as the content and significance of baptism are concerned.

John: I begin to realize that our doctrine of baptism may not be as Biblical as I formerly thought. However, I would like to have more light on the relationship between infant baptism and salvation.

3. INFANT BAPTISM AND SALVATION

Martin: Do you believe that all men are sinful and lost when they are born into this world? In other words, do infants need salvation in Christ?

John: Every member of the human race, without exception, possesses a corrupted nature, which is a source of actual sin, and is itself sin. By "nature" I mean that which is born in man, that which he has by birth. That there is an inborn corrupt state, from which sinful acts and dispositions flow, is evident from the sixth chapter of Luke, verses forty-three to forty-five: "There is no good tree that bringeth forth corrupt fruit . . . The evil man out of the evil treasure [of his heart] bringeth forth that which is evil." In the fifty-eighth Psalm, verse three, we read, "The wicked are estranged from the womb; they go astray as soon as they be born, speaking lies." This corrupt nature belongs to man from the first moment of his being, as we read in the fifty-first Psalm, verse five: "Behold, I was shapen in iniquity; and in sin did my mother conceive me." Paul declares in Ephesians, second chapter, third verse, that all men are by nature children of wrath. These texts indicate that, first, sin is an inborn depravity of the heart of man, and second, because of this depravity, man is guilty and condemnable before God, and under His wrath. There is no exception; all are sinful and need salvation.[45]

Martin: I am glad to know that you have that kind of Scriptural understanding of the sin of man and of his need of salvation. Christ says to Nicodemus: "That which is born of flesh is flesh; and that which is born of the Spirit is spirit. Marvel not that I said unto thee, Ye must be born again." "Except a man be born anew, he cannot see the kingdom of God." [46]

According to your doctrine, infants cannot be born again since they are not able to understand the Gospel. Do you, then, believe that infants have no possibility of being saved? In my view, that is the only possible conclusion from the baptistic doctrine.

John: No, we do not believe that infants are lost. Those who die in their infancy are saved by the atonement of Christ.

Martin: Don't you believe that we sinners become partakers of the blessings of Christ's atonement through faith, in the new birth?

John: We do, but children are saved directly by the atonement of Christ.

Martin: Then you have two entirely different ways of salvation: infants and adults are alike sinful and lost. The adults are saved through faith and the new birth, but infants are saved without faith and without the new birth. How do you reconcile this doctrine of yours with the words of Christ which I quoted: all men are born of the flesh, and cannot enter into the kingdom of God without the new birth, or birth of water and the Spirit? Do you make these words of Christ null and void in the case of infants?

John: I don't want to reject any words of Christ, or the Bible, but I cannot understand how an infant can believe, as it is in-

capable of understanding the word of God. Repentance and
faith belong together. Man must be convicted of his sins, pray
for pardon, and believe the Gospel. "Faith cometh by hearing,
and hearing by the word of Christ." [47] You have two different
conceptions of coming to faith, one for the infants and another
for the grown-ups.

Martin: I admit that I do not understand how infants can
believe. The regular order is the one shown by you; one must
become a believer through repentance and faith in the Gospel.
But although I don't understand how babes can believe, I take
the words of Christ simply as they are. He says that infants receive the kingdom of God, and the Bible shows us no other way
by which the kingdom can be received except through faith. To
assume that the kingdom can be received without faith is to in-
dulge our own speculations, without Scriptural warrant.

The simple meaning of the words of Christ is that no man,
not even an infant, can be saved without being born of the water
and the Spirit. If we deny them water, or baptism, they are not
born of water; and being left without the first thing that belongs
to entering into the kingdom of God, they are left outside of it.
Thus by denying them baptism, we hinder them from coming to
Jesus and into His kingdom, acting directly against His plain
words.

John: What about the infants who die without baptism? According to your doctrine they are lost.

Martin: The Bible reveals to us nothing of the fate of infants
who die without baptism. In general, we think that Martin
Luther was right in saying: "Not lack of, but contempt for, the
sacrament condemns. I hope that when little children are denied
baptism without it being their own fault, and the command of
God and prayer are not despised, the kind and merciful God will
graciously remember them. Let their souls be left in the hands
of and at the will of their heavenly Father, who, as we know, is
merciful."

We cannot say more than this about infants who die without
baptism, for God has not seen fit to reveal anything on them in
His word. It seems to me that you reason something like this:
Unbaptized infants cannot be lost. Infants cannot be born again
because they cannot understand the Gospel. Therefore they must
be saved directly through the atoning work of Christ.

The first premise of this reasoning is a thing of which we know
nothing. Do you think that Christian doctrine can be based on
an assumption that has no basis in the word of God?

John: Of course not. I have never thought that our doctrine at this point is based on such faulty reasoning.

Martin: I respect your honesty. Let us, then, lay aside the whole question of the fate of unbaptized infants. We must build our doctrine from what Scripture says, not from what it does not say.

If infants are saved by God, in some exceptional way unknown to us, we cannot build anything on such an exception. The regular God-ordained way of salvation is that man must be born of water and the Spirit in order to enter into the kingdom of God. And the plainly expressed will of Christ is that infants must be brought into the kingdom of God.

An interesting fact is, as I already have pointed out, that the idea of new birth through baptism is not new in Christianity. The Synagogue taught that a new birth takes place in baptism when a proselyte enters through it into the divine covenant. Nicodemus knew well this terminology of the Synagogue, for he was a "teacher in Israel." When Jesus spoke to him of being born of water he naturally understood these words as a reference to baptism. This, too, is a proof that Jesus meant baptism in speaking of being born of water. In order to enter into the kingdom of God man must be baptized into the remission of sins and receive the Holy Spirit.

I repeat, according to the express will of Christ, infants are brought to Him and into His kingdom through baptism. Through it they become His disciples. Afterward they must be taught to observe all things that He has commanded us.

John: Infants cannot have a conscious repentance and faith in Christ. Don't you think that such a conscious conviction of sin and faith based on a personal experience of grace are necessary to all men? Or do you think that people who have been baptized as infants become true Christians by way of an unconscious gradual growth?

Martin: Those are good and pertinent questions, and I am glad you brought them up.

Infants receive in baptism the adoption of God's children, and are washed from the guilt of their inborn sin-corruption. They are taken into the kingdom of grace, into a new relationship to God through Christ. The Holy Spirit is present in baptism and in the infant does the work that is possible in that phase of its growth. God deals with men as persons, not as things. His work is not mechanical and magical.

The infant cannot, of course, have a conscious conviction of its sinfulness, neither can it have a conscious experience of the grace and salvation of God in Christ. It cannot consciously trust in Christ and surrender to Him. Its faith must be an unconscious faith, for Christ says that an infant can receive the kingdom of God, that is, have faith.

The meaning of baptism, however, is that *the baptized person should consciously repent, experience salvation in Christ, believe in Him as his personal Savior, and give his heart and life to Him.* When a person is baptized in infancy, these things must come to pass in his life after he has reached the age of discretion, just as in the Old Covenant those circumcised in their infancy had to have a conscious circumcision of their heart later, to love God above all things, to trust in Him, and obey Him. Infant circumcision and baptism are analogous in this respect too.

It is therefore necessary that every person baptized as a babe has a personal conscious experience of sin and grace, in order that the grace into which he has been taken in his infancy shall become to him a personally known and owned reality.

Although the baptistic doctrine of the meaning of baptism is wholly unscriptural, in their practical Christian work those who hold that view have often been more Scriptural than those who have practiced infant baptism. They have insisted on a personal conscious repentance and faith, or a real conversion, in the life of all people, and that is the reason why they have so many confessing Christians in their churches. Those who have practiced infant baptism, although their doctrine of baptism has been more Scriptural, have often neglected evangelism and even led people *to assume that they are true Christians and saved just because they have been baptized, although they have no living faith and knowledge of Christ, and do not follow Him,* which, of course, is a horrible deception and fatal error.

Those who claim to be the children of the Evangelical Reformation, and regard the reformers as their fathers in that sense, have often failed to follow their teachings. Both Luther and Calvin teach that baptism does not save without a true personal faith and knowledge of Christ, for without it the meaning of baptism is not fulfilled in a person's life. Luther says in his *Small Catechism* that baptism "worketh forgiveness of sins, delivers from death and the devil, and confers everlasting salvation on all who believe, as the word and promise of God declare . . . It is not the water indeed that produces these effects, but the word of God, . . . and our faith which relies on the word of God . . ." Calvin says in his *Institutes:* "Baptism is not sanctified to us except by the word of promise received in faith . . . being blind and unbelieving for a long time, we did not embrace the promise which had been given us in baptism; yet . . . the promise itself, as it was from God, always remained steady, firm, and true . . . We confess, therefore, that during that time we received no advantage whatever from baptism, because we totally neglected the promise offered to us in it . . . Now, since, by the grace of God, we have begun to repent, we accuse our blindness and hardness of heart for our long ingratitude to His great goodness; yet we believe that the promise itself never expired, but, on the contrary, we reason in the following manner: By baptism God promises remission of sins, and will certainly fulfill the promise to all believers: that promise was offered to us in baptism; let us, therefore, embrace it by faith: it was long dormant by reason of our unbelief; now, then, let us receive it by faith." [48]

Both Luther and Calvin have the Scriptural view that God's promise and covenant in baptism is steady, firm, and true, whether a person believes or not, for God does not cease to be true if men are faithless. Both teach that baptism brings blessings and salvation only to those who believe in the Gospel. *In its actual spiritual sense the new birth takes place through faith, and only believers are truly born-again people. Only in them the meaning of baptism is fulfilled.* Unbelievers have not experienced and appropriated the saving grace, or have fallen from it. They do not live in it, but have turned away from it. Luther says that Abraham, Moses, Isaac, Gideon, and David were born-again believers, although they never were baptized, whereas unbelieving church members are unregenerate although they have been baptized.[49] Luther describes the way in which faith is born in grown-up people as follows:

"When the penitent and terrified conscience attains peace, consolation and joy from this Gospel, it is called faith. This faith justifies us before God. People must be diligently instructed that this faith cannot be born without serious and true repentance and terror of conscience before God. . . . This must be continually emphasized in order that people would not fall into self-deceit and assume that they have faith although they are far from it. . . . For true faith must bring with it consolation and joy toward God. Such a consolation and joy cannot be felt where a person has no contrition and terror, as Christ says . . . 'The Gospel is preached to the poor.' " [50]

These words do not apply to those alone who have fallen to unbelief. They also apply to such people who have been religious from their childhood, and have not fallen into an overtly worldly and sinful life. They, too, must come to know sin and grace in an experienced way in order that the meaning of baptism may be fulfilled in them. In this way their repentance and faith, which was unconscious when they were baptized as infants, becomes a conscious repentance and faith.

John: I am glad for your emphasis on evangelism and the necessity of an experienced repentance and faith. But when you speak of an unconscious and conscious repentance and faith, don't you use these terms in two wholly different meanings, and thus run into contradiction? How can a person repent and believe unconsciously?

Martin: If I were to think of that matter according to my reason I would admit that you are right. But I do not want to be led by my natural reason but by the word of God. Christ says that infants can receive the kingdom of God. Since the kingdom of God can be received only by repentance and faith, infants must be able to have repentance and faith. It is, however, obvious that they cannot have it consciously.[51] The Bible also teaches that all men should repent and believe in a conscious manner. This applies to those, too, who have been baptized as infants. The only possible conclusion that I see is that they must have a conscious repentance and faith when they come to the age of discretion, and that the meaning of baptism is so fulfilled in them.

What I said applies, naturally, only to those extremely few cases in which people do not fall from grace, but remain godly from their childhood. The great majority of people fall from grace to unbelief and sinful life, and they must, of course, repent and believe the Gospel. Do you have any better explanation of this matter, if you take seriously the words of Christ that infants are able to receive the kingdom of God, and that all men should repent and believe the Gospel?

John: I guess I don't. But isn't it largely due to infant baptism that true evangelism is so often neglected and even opposed in churches which practice it? It seems to me that the leaders of our denomination are largely justified in saying that infant baptism is responsible for sending more people to hell than any other cause. Isn't it a dreadful thing to baptize a baby and let him grow up believing that by baptism he has been saved and is on his way to heaven, although he knows nothing of an experienced repentance and faith?[52] It seems to me that the evil effects of infant baptism are a strong argument against it. It leads people to a superstitious confidence in an outward rite as possessed of regenerating efficacy, and destroys the Church as a spiritual body, by merging it in the nation and the world.[53]

Martin: It's true that there is a great amount of false reliance on baptism. But I do not believe that that is the fault of infant baptism, which is clearly based on the teachings of the New Testament, particularly of Christ. Infant baptism in itself is a good and gracious institution. Referring to the words of Peter, "The promise is unto you and your children," [54] Calvin says aptly, "It ought to be admitted . . . beyond all controversy that God is so kind and liberal to his servants as . . . to appoint even the children who shall descend from them to be enrolled among his people." [55] The fact that there is much false reliance on baptism received in infancy is not the fault of the baptism but of a false teaching. People have a tendency to use all possible ideas in their excuse mechanism against personal repentance and salvation. But when the word of God is preached in the power of the Holy Spirit, and with the purpose of leading people to a conscious repentance and faith, infant baptism has proved to be no hindrance. On the contrary, it has proved to be advantageous. Recently a pastor who has done evangelistic work both among Baptists and Pedobaptists told me that, according to his experience, people are more easily converted among the Pedobaptists. Work among them is more hopeful.

Don't you think that Gospel preaching, as an ordinance of Christ, should be always practiced and maintained in the Church?

John: Of course, it should. Why do you ask such a question?

Martin: I suppose you know as well as I do that in the sphere of Christendom the wrong kind of preaching and teaching has sent more people to hell than any other human cause. Don't you think that it would be better to stop all the preaching in the churches, because most of it is harmful from the point of view of salvation?

John: Don't make fun of me. I suppose you mean that a good thing can be misused, and that this misuse and its harmful effects are no valid reason for abandoning the whole thing.

Martin: Exactly. I have tried to show that infant baptism is based on the express will and plain words of Christ, and as such it is a good gift of God. The Lord's Supper too is misused. But the fact that most people receive it in a wrong way, without true faith, would not justify its abandonment.

If we wish to be obedient to the plain teachings of Christ, we must baptize the babes of Christian people. But at the same time we should teach that *all people who have received baptism in their infancy should have a personal experience of sin and grace, and receive the Holy Spirit in a definite and experienced way. Only so can a person have a true saving knowledge of Christ as his Savior and power to follow Him and live for Him.*

John: I agree with what you said in your last statement. But it seems to me that your church, and the churches practicing infant baptism in general, do not so believe or teach in practice. The pastors of these churches seem to assume that the young people who have been baptized as infants are Christians, born-again people, when they come to confirmation instruction, although most of them have no life in God in them. It seems to me that the coercion in Sunday and Confirmation schools to get children and young people to heed the word is because they do not truly have life in faith. Anyone born of God loves the Lord and His word and the things of God, and does not need such coercing. Infant baptism seems to have led most pastors *to deal with unbelievers as though they were believers.* The same holds true of the adult church members. If they go to church and lead a decent life they are assumed to be Christians, although they have no clear witness of the Spirit either by mouth or life.

Martin: I admit that you are right in most of what you have said. A sad fact is that so many pastors do not divide the word of God aright, giving to each person the share of it that belongs to him. Perhaps the most horrible deception and error that a pastor can make is to treat an unbeliever and unregenerate person as a Christian and so confirm him in his walk on the way which leads to destruction. The word of God should be rightly divided, so that unbelievers would be dealt with as unbelievers, convicted sinners as convicted sinners, and believers as believers. No medical doctor would mix together all medicines and give the same concoction to all his patients, without regard to their condition and need. Nevertheless, this is what most ministers do. The right division of the word of God is rare. An unregenerate pastor may teach a formally correct doctrine, but he will never be able to divide the word of God aright. Therefore he will always mislead people, as Christ says: If the blind lead the blind, they will both fall into the pit. Sad to say, it is quite common that in our time people believe that a spiritually blind pastor can lead his flock in the way of life if he knows the correct doctrine, or that God will lead people to faith through the ministry of a spiritually blind pastor. This means that these people do not think Christ was right in saying that when the blind leads the blind they will both fall into the pit, the pit of damnation.

John: I agree. But I have another question for you. Most people who have been baptized as infants live as unbelievers, and their baptism does not seem to have any real significance to them. How would you explain this fact?

4. Falling from Grace and the Return to It

Martin: It is true that the great majority of people who have been baptized in their infancy are unbelievers and travel on the broad way which leads to destruction. But that is not the fault of infant baptism. The reasons lie elsewhere. Most people die in bed, but that is not usually the fault of their bed. Many people die of overeating; that is, however, not the fault of food, but of its misuse. A thing must be good in itself before it can be misused.

In the Apostolic Age and after it, only children of Christian homes were baptized. According to Christ's instruction, the baptized were to be taught to know His commands and follow them. Only in Christian homes was that possible.

In our time, infant baptism is used too indiscriminately. Infants are baptized even when there is little, if any, guarantee of a Christian rearing. Such a practice is a departure from the principles followed in the early Church. A child who grows up in an unbelieving and perhaps overtly worldly and ungodly home has hardly any chance to come to a conscious and personal knowledge of the Savior to whom he was brought in baptism.

Even when baptized children live in Christian homes, many of them fall from grace. You know from the New Testament what a large proportion of people who were converted as adults fell away and lost Christ. Some have estimated that almost half—and sometimes more than a half—of the people converted in the great revivals of our time fail to continue in faith to the end, although they receive Christian care and nurture in the Church. Is it any wonder, then, that children who receive no Christian nurture go to the world and become unbelievers?

John: I must disagree with you with regard to the falling from grace. I know that your church teaches that a person can be saved and then fall from grace and be lost forever, unless he is converted again and so restored to grace. But that is not what Scripture teaches. You remember the words of Christ:

"My sheep hear my voice, and I know them, and they follow

me: and I give unto them eternal life; and they shall never perish, and no one shall snatch them out of my hand. My Father, who hath given them unto me, is greater than all; and no one is able to snatch them out of the Father's hand." [56]

Again He says: "And this is the Father's will who hath sent me that of all which he hath given me I should lose nothing, but should raise it up again at the last day. And this is the will of him that sent me, that everyone which seeth the Son, and believeth on him, may have everlasting life: and I shall raise him up at the last day." [57]

You also know the words of Paul: "For I am persuaded that neither death, nor life, nor angels, nor principalities, nor powers, nor things present, nor things to come, nor height, nor depth, nor any other creature, shall be able to separate us from the love of God, which is in Christ Jesus our Lord." [58]

And He said also: "For whom he did foreknow he also did predestinate to be conformed to the image of his Son . . . Moreover whom he did predestinate, them he also called; and whom he called, them he also justified: and whom he justified, them he also glorified." [59]

These statements of Christ and Paul teach quite plainly that a person who is once saved through faith in Christ will never be lost again. "They shall never perish." God has glorified every person whom he foreknew, predestinated, called, and justified. The doctrine that a saved person can fall from grace and be lost is based on the view that salvation depends to some extent on man and his ability to endure to the end. Scripture teaches that as salvation is by grace, without any merit and work of ours, so is perseverance wholly a work of God. Paul says, God "shall also confirm you to the end, that ye be blameless in the day of our Lord Jesus Christ. God is faithful, by whom ye were called unto the fellowship of his Son Jesus Christ." [60] Peter says likewise that Christians "are kept by the power of God through faith unto salvation ready to be revealed in the last time." [61] John writes in the same tone: "Beloved, now we are sons of God, and it doeth not yet appear what we shall be: but we know that, when he shall appear, we shall be like him; for we shall see him as he is." [62] All the children of God will be kept by the power of God—not by their own power—to eternal salvation, and they all know that they will be like Christ when He shall appear.

There are people who seem to be Christians but are not truly saved. They are like the foolish virgins who have the form of godliness and associate with true Christians but are not true believers, having no oil in their vessels. Christ says: "Not every one that saith unto me, Lord, Lord, shall enter into the kingdom of heaven; but he that doeth the will of my Father which is in heaven. Many will say to me in that day, Lord, Lord, have we not prophesied in thy name? and in thy name cast out devils? and in thy name done many wonderful works? And then will I profess unto them, I never knew you: depart from me, ye that work iniquity." [63]

These words of Christ show that people may have professed Christianity, they may have been very active in what is called Christian work, they may have accomplished many wonderful works, but the Lord has never known them as His own. He does not say: I used to know you, but you have forfeited my favor and fallen from grace, and I do not know you any longer. He says: "I never knew you."

Christ's parable of the sower shows that the seed may fall on rocky ground where it has but little earth, springing up soon but soon withering away, so are many people influenced by the Gospel superficially, but their hearts remain unchanged; or the thorns of sin remain in their hearts and choke the word, and they never become true believers. If infants were truly saved in baptism, they would never fall away. The fact that most of them never are true Christians shows that they have never been truly saved.

Martin: I know the doctrine of eternal security, according to which a person once saved is always saved. I have studied carefully two books defending this doctrine, H. A. Ironside's *The Eternal Security of the Believer* [64] and J. F. Strombeck's *Shall Never Perish,* [65] and have deeply enjoyed much that they say. The statements of Christ and the apostles that you quoted are blessed promises which are fully trustworthy, as all the word of God is. I agree with you, and with Ironside and Strombeck, in the understanding that salvation is wholly by grace, a work of God from the beginning to the end. It is God who works both to will and to do in all things that pertain to salvation. It is by His power that we are saved and preserved. We are wholly condemned, helpless and lost in ourselves, and wholly at God's mercy in the matter of salvation.

Still, as I see it, the doctrine of eternal security is only one line of truth found in the Scriptures. The other line of Scriptural teaching points in the direction of the possibility, or serious danger, of being lost, even if a person has once been truly saved. I cannot understand otherwise the words of Paul in the eleventh chapter of Romans, verses nineteen to twenty-two, which say:

"Thou wilt say then, the branches were broken off, that I might be grafted in. Well; because of unbelief they were broken off, and thou standest by faith. Be not highminded but fear: for if God spared not the natural branches, take heed lest he also spare not thee. Behold therefore the goodness and severity of God: on them which fell, severity; but toward thee, goodness, if thou continue in his goodness: otherwise thou also shalt be cut off."

Paul speaks here to Gentile Christians. They will obtain eternal salvation if they continue in the goodness of God. Otherwise they shall be cut off. If the doctrine "once saved, always saved" were true, these words would be senseless, as no saved person would be "cut off" from Christ.

The Lord Himself says about the same thing: "If a man abide not in me, he is cast off as a branch, and is withered; and men gather them, and cast them into the fire, and they are burned." [66] It is possible to speak of abiding in Christ only if one is grafted in Him by faith, that is, if he is saved. Of such a person Christ says that he may fail to abide in Him, and will be rejected and cast into fire. If the doctrine "once saved, always saved" were true, Christ hardly could have spoken thus, since, according to that doctrine, every saved person abides in Christ and will never be cast off. Strombeck explains that Christ does not speak here of truly saved people.[67] But I do not see how one can abide in Christ unless he is saved. Christ says another time: "He that shall endure to the end shall be saved." [68] This statement, too, would be senseless if every believer would endure to the end. Strombeck explains that Christ speaks in these words only of the Israelites, and that the words cannot be applied to Christians.[69] Such a distinction is, however, wholly unwarranted, for in the matter of salvation there is no difference between the Jews and Gentiles.[70]

Paul writes: "Now the Spirit speaketh expressly, that in the latter times some shall depart from the faith, giving heed to seducing spirits, and doctrines of devils." [71] The apostle says here clearly that some Christians shall depart from the faith. Strombeck explains that this passage does not speak of the individual's faith in the Savior for salvation, but of the true doctrine. The New Testament does not speak of faith in the sense of true doctrine alone, but personal saving faith and true doctrine belong together. Paul means that some Christians will depart from both.

In Hebrews, sixth chapter, fourth to sixth verses, we read: "For it is impossible for those who were once enlightened, and have tasted of the heavenly gift, and were made partakers of the Holy Ghost, and have tasted the good word of God, and the powers of the world to come, if they shall fall away, to renew them again unto repentance; seeing they crucify to themselves the Son of God afresh, and put him to an open shame."

Those who hold the doctrine of eternal security explain that this passage does not speak of truly saved people. However, if a person who is a partaker of the Holy Spirit, that is, has the Holy Spirit dwelling in him, is not saved, I do not really know who is. The word "taste" is used also of a genuine Christian experience of grace.[72] Christians who have had a genuine experience (taste) of salvation and have received the Holy Spirit may fall away. The words that they cannot be renewed to repentance probably refer to cases in which the fallen persons really "crucify to themselves the Son of God afresh, and put him to an open shame," that is, who become overt and hardened enemies of Christianity and commit the sin against the Holy Spirit, treading under foot the Son of God, counting His blood an unholy thing and doing despite (reviling, mocking, in the Greek sense of the word) the Spirit of grace, as the same sacred writer says later on.[73]

If we finally think of such parables of the Lord as those of the lost sheep, the lost coin, and the prodigal son,[74] they do not make sense if the doctrine of eternal security is true. In these parables the shepherd lost a sheep that was in his flock, the woman lost the coin she possessed, and the son left his father and home. The sheep was found again, and so was the coin, and the son returned. All these parables contain the idea that a person who is truly the Lord's own can be lost by falling from grace, and then be restored to it, or return to it by repentance. The doctrine of eternal security denies that the sheep was ever really *in* the shepherd's flock, or that it ever was really lost, or that the son ever was really *in* his father's house, or that he ever became really a prodigal.

If we were to follow the method of those who teach the doctrine of eternal security, we could "prove," for instance, that all men will finally be saved, and none will ultimately be lost, since the Bible says that God wills the salvation of all men, and that He is able to accomplish all that He wills. Paul says that God will "gather together in one in heaven, and which are on earth; even in him." [75] None will be excluded; all will be saved. Nevertheless, the Bible teaches that many people will be eternally lost. Likewise, the Bible teaches that Christ's own shall never perish; and yet some believers will fall away from grace and lose Christ.[76] We must take both lines of Biblical teaching as they are, although we cannot harmonize them in a logical way. Faith lives in the tension between these two: confident reliance on the grace and keeping power of God, and in the fear of falling away. The reality of this danger drives the Christian to put his trust in the mercy and keeping power of the Lord, to watch and pray, to practice self-discipline by the power of the Spirit, lest he become a castaway, as Paul says,[77] to condemn his sins and faults and repent of them, trusting in the forgiveness of God for Christ's sake. The danger of falling away is not on the side of God but on our side, and in the fact that the devil walks around as a roaring lion, seeking whom he may devour. The danger and possibility of a fall does not, as Strombeck thinks, lead to reliance on one's own power and efforts. On the contrary, when rightly understood, it causes the Christian to give up all self-reliance and to depend wholly on the mercy and keeping power of God. It helps the Christian to be realistic with regard to the situation in which he lives, and to trust in grace alone, both for justification and sanctification, for salvation and preservation.

John: I must admit that the passages you quoted seem to speak against the doctrine of eternal security. Let us assume that it is possible to fall away, and that many baptized persons actually have fallen from grace. Experience shows, however, that when the Gospel work is done among baptized unbelievers, they are in no way different from unbaptized unbelievers. How do you explain this fact?

Martin: An unbeliever is an unbeliever, whether he has been baptized or not. He is in an unregenerate state even though he once has been baptized. In one respect unbaptized unbelievers, however, differ from those who have been baptized: the former are in reality heathen, but baptized unbelievers are prodigal sons and daughters. They have once been in the heavenly Father's house but have then left it and live in the distant land of sin and unbelief. When the former are converted, they must be baptized unto the forgiveness of their sins and receive the Holy Spirit. When the latter are converted they do not need a new baptism, for the New Testament never tells that baptized people who fell away and then returned were baptized again.

John: How do you understand the conversion of a person who has been baptized in his infancy?

Martin: Christ shows the simple way into His kingdom when He says: "The kingdom of God is at hand: repent ye and believe in the gospel." [78] He gave His disciples the command that "repentance and remission of sins should be preached in his name unto all the nations." [79]

Preaching of repentance means that unconcerned sinners are convicted of their sins and their lost condition by means of the law and called to a godly sorrow for them. To those who humble themselves to be sorry for their sins and to beg for mercy, the Gospel of God's free pardon in the all-sufficient sacrifices of Christ and in His resurrection-victory must be proclaimed, both in public sermons and in personal counselling.

The Gospel is the key whereby the gate of the kingdom of grace is opened to repenting sinners, and by means of which they are helped to enter in by faith. When they are under conviction and pray for pardon and salvation they are knocking at the door. When they believe the Gospel that promises them forgiveness and free justification in Christ's blood they enter in.

Faith does not only mean trust in pardon in Christ. It also means surrender to His rule in willing obedience to His will. The Holy Spirit works this faith by means of the Gospel.

In the case of *unbaptized* people, baptism is the external sacred act by which the Gospel promise is "sealed" to repenting sinners. The internal sealing is done by the Spirit. In the case of *baptized* people, the laying on of hands may be used when the Gospel assurance of forgiveness and the promise of the Holy Spirit is proclaimed to them. In the Apostolic Church this sacred act was used in various kinds of blessing, and in connection with it the Holy Spirit was frequently received, as we have seen. The same thing happens often in our time. The Gospel is, of course, equally sure and reliable without the laying on of hands, yet this sacred rite "seals" or confirms it externally and helps to believe it. The inward sealing is, of course, always given by the Spirit.

There are many people who receive an assurance of salvation while listening to a sermon, and some receive comfort while reading a Christian book. But even in their case a personal assurance of the promise of forgiveness and the Holy Spirit with the laying on of hands is beneficial for the confirmation of their faith, and for tying them more closely to the Church, the body of Christ, and through it the Holy Spirit is often given for a living knowledge of Christ and power from on high.

John: I know that some churches use the laying on of hands, but I do not understand why it should be used.

Martin: Its use is no law. It is a privilege, a help to our faith. We should appreciate and gratefully use all the sacred acts practiced by the apostles. Let us remember that many people at that time did not receive the Holy Spirit until they were blessed by the laying on of hands. The same is true in our time, for the ways of God have not changed. Besides, in the sixth chapter of Hebrews, first and second verses, the laying on of hands is listed among the principles, or first and fundamental things, of the doctrine of Christ, along with repentance from dead works, faith in God, the doctrine of baptisms (water and Spirit baptism), resurrection of the dead, and eternal judgment. If we omit one of these principles that belong to the foundation, a part of the foundation is lacking.

The main thing, however, is not anything that is done externally. It is essential that we hear the Gospel, but it is still more important that we grasp it by faith and internally experience its power, being "circumcised" in our hearts to faith and obedience, or, in other words, receive the internal baptism of the Holy Spirit.

Sad to say, it is quite common in churches practicing infant baptism to lay emphasis on pure doctrine and external "churchianity." There is no call to conversion, devoted Christian life, and consecrated service. All that is required is that one learn his catechism, attend church services, partake of the Lord's Supper, contribute to the work of the church, and lead a decent life. All this is, of course, good and necessary; but a person may well have all that and still be entirely void of true knowledge of Christ and life in Him. When people are allowed to assume that they are Christians and heirs of eternal life without true repentance and faith, they are actually led to build up their own righteousness, and will finally be condemned.

John: I agree with you in the main. A living heart-knowledge of Christ, and life in and for Him, is, after all, the main thing.

Martin: The history of the Christian Church shows that living Christianity and revivals do not decisively depend on the use of infant baptism or adult baptism. It depends on the way the word of God is preached. Scriptural evangelistic preaching and personal soul-winning result in revivals and produce living Christianity. Unevangelistic, cold and formal preaching, as well as modernistic watered-down teaching, produces spiritual death and formal churchliness.

Most of the great revivals of the Christian Church have occurred in denominations which practice infant baptism. Such were, for instance, the major part of the evangelical Reformation Movement in the sixteenth century, the so-called Pietistic revivals of the seventeenth, eighteenth and nineteenth centuries in many European countries and America, the Moravian and Methodistic revivals, the major part of the Great Awakening in America, the Finney and Moody revivals, and others. True, great revivals have taken place through the antipedobaptists too, but there is no question of the fact that the major part of living Christianity has always been in churches that have practiced infant baptism. On the other hand, rejection of infant baptism has not prevented a part of American Baptism from becoming modernistic and losing its life. It seems to me that opposition to infant baptism has been a hindrance rather than an advantage in the work for the salvation of men.

Let us think of a Lutheran, Methodist, Anglican (Episcopalian), or Presbyterian person who is touched in his conscience while attending a revivalistic meeting conducted by a church that opposes infant baptism. He feels that he should repent and be converted. He has his difficulties, as all men have, but to the others is added this one: if he were to follow the invitation and heed the call of God in the meeting, he probably would have to repudiate as worthless and wrong the baptism that he has received in his infancy. He would also have to leave his own church which practices infant baptism.

These considerations hinder many people from being converted through the work done by churches or groups which reject infant baptism. I am also convinced that God bestows His richest blessings upon an evangelistic or revivalistic work that is done in complete faithfulness to His word, including the doctrine of baptism.

John: I have never thought of these things from that angle. It is customary among us to blame infant baptism for the spiritual deadness of other churches. Maybe that conception is wrong.

5. "Who Can Forgive Sins but God Only?"

Martin: I am glad we are in close agreement on many issues. Since we are discussing conversion, I would like to take up the question of absolution, since your pastor recently talked on it over the radio. He referred to the words in Mark, second chapter, seventh verse: "Who can forgive sins but God only?" On the basis of these words he asserted that it is wrong to declare absolution to penitent sinners. We can only direct him to ask God to forgive his sins, he said. Declaration of absolution is popery, Catholicism. Do you have the same conception as your pastor?

John: I do. Aren't the words plain? "Who can forgive sins but
God only?" These words plainly refute the doctrine held not only
by Catholics, but also by Lutherans and Episcopalians, that men
can remit sins, and that through absolution they pronounce sins
forgiven before God in heaven. I think that such a doctrine and
practice is horrible heresy.

Martin: Do you think that all the statements in the Bible are
to be followed by us?

John: Of course not. The Bible contains words of ungodly
people and even of the devil. Scripture certainly does not intend
that we should follow such words. An example of this type is the
assertion of the fool, "There is no God." [80]

Martin: You're right, brother. But you have probably never
paid attention to the fact that the words "Who can forgive sins
but God only" were spoken by some scribes who belonged to the
party of the Pharisees. You are using a statement of the Pharisaic
scribes for the foundation of your doctrine. And when you follow
a doctrine of the Pharisees, what do you yourselves become?

John: When the scribes said those words against Christ, denying His power to remit sins, they did not realize and believe that
God was in Him, and that He had power on earth to forgive
sins. But no other man has similar power.

Martin: You have probably forgotten that Christ gave such a
power to His disciples when He said to them after His resurrection: "As the Father hath sent me, even so send I you . . .
Receive ye the Holy Ghost: whose soever sins ye remit, they are
remitted (R.V. forgive . . . forgiven) unto them; whose soever
sins ye retain, they are retained." [81]

That was not the only time the Lord spoke to His disciples of
the power to remit sins. When Peter had confessed Him as Christ,
the Son of God, Jesus said to him, "I will give unto thee the
keys of the kingdom of heaven: and whatsoever thou shalt bind
on earth shall be bound in heaven: and whatsoever thou shalt
loose on earth shall be loosed in heaven." [82]

The Lord spoke to Peter as a representative of all His disciples.
We know this from the fact that a little later He said essentially
the same thing to the other disciples: "Verily, I say unto you,
Whatsoever ye shall bind on earth shall be bound in heaven: and
whatsoever ye shall loose on earth shall be loosed in heaven." [83]

"To bind" means obviously the same thing as "to retain sins";
and "to loose" means the same as "to remit (forgive) sins."
Christ has given this power to all His disciples, those who have
the Holy Spirit.

John: He said those words to His apostles, and I think that power was given to them only, not to others.

Martin: In the twentieth chapter of John we read that the disciples were behind the locked doors, not that the apostles only were there. The words were said to *disciples,* not merely to the apostles. Those who deny that the disciples, Christians, have power to remit sins have the same view as the scribes and Pharisees who said, "Who can forgive sins but God only?" As they did not believe that God was in Christ, so you do not believe that God, and Christ, is in Christians. Still, the Bible teaches plainly that God, Christ, and the Holy Spirit, the triune God, is in Christians. It is truly God, or Christ, who forgives sins; but being in the Christians, He speaks through their mouths and remits sins through their agency.

John: We do not deny that the triune God dwells in Christians. We know well that the New Testament speaks of it many times.

Martin: You admit it in theory, but deny it in practice. Christ said to His disciples: "He that heareth you heareth me; and he that despiseth you despiseth me." [84] He who hears the Gospel promise of forgiveness from the mouth of a disciple of Christ hears it from Christ. It is He who speaks through the disciple's mouth. You despise and reject the word of forgiveness, or absolution, spoken by Christ's disciples. In doing so you despise Christ.

John: Certainly not. We simply do not presume to take from Christ and God the honor of having the sole right to forgive sins.

Martin: The best way to give glory to Christ is to believe and obey His words. We honor Him by taking Him at His word, "Whose soever sins ye remit they are remitted to him." You dishonor Him by refusing to believe these words and to follow them by remitting sins to penitent sinners. Paul says, "Now then we are ambassadors for Christ, as though God did beseech you by us." [85] Let us assume that a king asks a man to be his ambassador and to convey to someone a given message. The man refuses to do so, explaining that he cannot, and demands that the king do it in person. Don't you think that by his behavior he dishonors his king and well deserves the king's anger? In the same way you refuse to declare to people God's forgiveness, although Christ commands you to do so as His ambassadors. Christ instructs His disciples to preach repentance and forgiveness in His name, and to remit sins to penitent sinners. But in your pretended humility you decline obedience to Christ. Instead of proclaiming the remission of sins to burdened and grace-seeking souls, you direct them to pray and surrender to God, or something like that. And you also yourselves refuse to ask for and to receive the absolution from a servant of Christ, since you do not believe that Christ Himself speaks through him as His ambassador.

John: Don't be too hard on us. The apostles never speak of absolution in their letters; neither does the book of Acts say anything about it. You use the laying on of hands in declaring forgiveness of sins, but according to the Acts this usage was practiced in order that people might receive the Holy Spirit. The fact that the apostles do not speak of absolution in their letters shows that it was not used in the Apostolic Church.

Martin: The records of the life of Christ and His teachings which we have in our Gospels were the chief contents of apostolic teaching and preaching, both in missionary work and in congregations. According to the Gospels, Christ spoke four times of the task and power to proclaim forgiveness of sins, or to remit sins. The fact that these words of Christ are recorded in the Gospels shows that they were regarded as important parts of the Lord's teaching, and they were repeatedly inculcated in Christians. I believe that the teaching of Christ is quite sufficient to establish a Christian doctrine. You seem to think that unless a doctrine is taught in apostolic epistles, Christ's words mean nothing.

John: That accusation is not fair. We certainly believe that the teachings of Christ are divine truth.

Martin: You do so in theory but not in practice. The epistles of the apostles were written for definite purposes. The apostles dealt in them with matters which caused difficulties in the churches. If there had not been disturbances in the celebration of the Lord's Supper in the church of Corinth, this sacrament would not be mentioned at all in the apostolic letters.

It is not true that the declaration of forgiveness, or absolution, is not mentioned in apostolic epistles. In Second Corinthians, chapter two, Paul exhorts the Corinthian Christians to forgive a man his sins, assuring that he also was willing to forgive. "To whom ye forgive anything, I forgive also: for if I forgave anything, to whom I forgave it, for your sakes forgave I it in the person of Christ."

John: Christians should naturally forgive those who have offended them. This was probably such a case.

Martin: Paul writes of the same man in the fifth chapter of First Corinthians. He was a Christian who had committed a sin of gross fornication. His sin was not against the Corinthian Christians or Paul personally, just as David's sin was not against Nathan. But as God declared forgiveness to the penitent David through Nathan, so this fallen Corinthian Christian was to be forgiven through the Corinthian Christians. He was penitent, and the members of the Corinthian Church had to forgive him; so also did Paul in the person or name of Christ. In my view, here is a clear case of the use of the Christ-given task and power to remit sins to a penitent sinner. It is done "in the person of Christ," in His name and as His representatives. Christ is in His own, and He speaks through their mouths; therefore forgiveness takes place "in the person of Christ."

You said that the laying on of hands was used in order that people would receive the Holy Spirit. It was also used in various kinds of blessing, as in healing the sick, in ordaining for ministry, or in imparting the spiritual blessings of the kingdom of God in general, as when Jesus blessed the children. Remission of sins is a blessing, and consequently the laying on of hands should be used in connection with it. Forgiveness of sins and the gift of the Holy Spirit are very closely united in the New Covenant. The divine pardon cannot be truly appropriated without the gift of the Holy Spirit. And when the gift of the Spirit is received, forgiveness is truly grasped in faith. I do not understand why we should emphasize their difference with regard to the use of the laying on of hands. Nevertheless, the declaration of the forgiveness of sins, or absolution, is valid even without the laying on of hands. This sacred act is not essential in absolution, but its use in it is quite right and proper.

John: But don't we assume for ourselves the prerogatives of God and Christ when we declare the forgiveness of sins? We may declare the forgiveness of sins, but we can hardly say that we remit sins.

Martin: I already said that there is no presumption in obedience to the words of Christ. There is a story of a French king who asked one of his officials to enter into a carriage before him. The official did so without hesitation. The other members of the king's retinue were horrified because of such disrespect, as they thought. But the king rewarded the official, declaring that he was best honored by obedience.

It is presumption to disobey Christ or to explain that He does not mean what He says. He said to His disciples: "Verily, verily I say unto you, He that believeth on me, the works that I do shall he do also; and greater works than these shall he do; because I go unto my Father." [86] Christ declared remission of sins when He was here on earth. He said on one occasion: "Son, be of good cheer; thy sins be forgiven thee." [87] After His going to the Father, His disciples do the same works as He did. They, too, say to penitent sinners: "Be of good cheer; thy sins are forgiven thee"; but they add: "In Jesus' name and His atoning blood," because Christ commanded His disciples to preach forgiveness in His name, and because the Bible teaches that we have redemption in His blood, the forgiveness of our sins, for the blood of Christ alone cleanses from all sin.[88]

In the Old Covenant the blood of animals was sprinkled upon sin-defiled people with a hyssop bundle. In the New Covenant the blood of Christ is sprinkled upon the hearts of penitent people by means of the Gospel. The New Testament speaks several times of the sprinkling of the blood of Christ. All true Christians have become partakers of this sprinkling.[89] It is done by Christians who are a holy priesthood unto God. The sprinkling of Christ's blood through the Gospel is received by faith. We have "our hearts sprinkled from an evil conscience"; we have come "to Jesus the mediator of the new covenant, and to the blood of sprinkling, that speaketh better things than that of Abel." [90] The elect of God are, Peter writes, sanctified by the Spirit "unto obedience and sprinkling of the blood of Jesus Christ." [91] Do you, brother John, know any other way in which the blood of Christ can be sprinkled on men and their hearts except by the proclamation of the Gospel?

John: I guess there is no other way.

Martin: You said a short while ago that in your view it is right to proclaim the Gospel of forgiveness to penitent sinners. Do you believe that this Gospel which we preach is true? In other words, is it acknowledged by God as true?

John: Of course, the Gospel is true when it is preached according to the Scriptures. But not all people are saved, even when the forgiveness of sins is proclaimed to them personally. Doesn't that show that our declaration of forgiveness and God's forgiveness are two different things? Sins are not always forgiven in heaven when they are forgiven on earth.

Martin: The Catholics say that the key, or absolution, may err, and that God's forgiveness is not the same as the remission declared here. At this point you seem to take the same position as the papists.

Christ says: "Whatsoever ye shall loose on earth shall be loosed in heaven." He does not say: What ye loose on earth may not be loosed in heaven, as you explain. He says unconditionally, it "shall be loosed in heaven." The forgiveness declared on earth is truly God's forgiveness.

We know well that not all believe the Gospel when it is preached publicly. Neither do all believe it when it is proclaimed in personal absolution. The personal absolution is actually only the promise of the Gospel applied to one person individually. We cannot give faith and the Holy Spirit. God must give them.

You remember the parable in which Christ speaks of four different grounds on which the seed of God's word falls. The seed, the word, is the same, but it cannot grow and bring forth fruit unless man's heart is "good ground." And that is the case only in few people. There are people who seem to be repenting, but actually are not. Some people who appear to be penitent have some hidden sin that they are not able to confess. It seems too shameful to them, or they do not want to forsake it, and so they are not able to appropriate the grace which is declared to them. The promise is true, for the Gospel is divine truth. It is truly God's forgiveness; but they are not able to receive it. Sometimes it happens that a person grasps in faith the forgiveness that has been proclaimed to him later, after some hours, days, weeks, or sometimes even a longer period. God gives power to believe and seals the Gospel to the heart when He sees fit, and when the heart has become prepared for it.

Your pastor said in his speech that our doctrine and practice of absolution is an ecclesiastical tradition that has come from the Catholic Church. In reality your rejection of it is a false ecclesiastical tradition, and by it you make of no effect the teaching of Christ. You remember how the Lord said to the Pharisees of His time: "Ye have made void the word of God because of your tradition. Ye hypocrites, well did Isaiah prophesy of you, saying, This people honoreth me with their lips, but their heart is far from me. But in vain do they worship me, teaching as their doctrines the precepts of men." [92]

Because of your tradition you make void the plain words of Christ, and teach human precepts as your doctrine. Our doctrine and practice is based on the simple teaching of the word of God. It is not a Romish doctrine and practice, for, as you know, the Church of Rome teaches that only the ordained priests have power to declare remission of sins; but we teach, following the words of Christ, that all Christians, those who have the Holy Spirit, have the Christ-given task and power to declare the Gospel of forgiveness to those who repent and seek grace. Christ says:

"Ask, and it shall be given you." Forgiveness in the name and redemptive blood of Christ is given in the Gospel or absolution to
those who penitently ask for it.

John: Can't we say that when a repentant sinner complies to
the God-prescribed prerequisites, that is, is sorry for his sins, prays
for pardon, desires to be rid of sin, and puts his trust in Christ's
atoning sacrifice, he is automatically free because of the promise
which is in the Scriptures—just as an impenitent sinner is bound
to his sins and hellbound by the judgment of the word of God?

Martin: Let's take an illustration. A criminal sentenced to
death asks for pardon, and the king grants it. When the document
by which the pardon and full freedom is granted is signed, the
criminal is free—but only in principle and in theory. It is necessary that an official go to him and proclaim the pardon to him,
show him the letter signed by the king, and open to him the
prison's gates. The penitent sinner has a letter of pardon from
the heavenly King, but it must be proclaimed to him by one of
the King's officials, and he must accept it. The official, of course,
has no power of his own to pardon the criminal. He acts as an
official or agent of the king. Likewise, the servant of God only
proclaims the pardon that the heavenly King has authorized him
to declare, and also shows that he does it on the basis of His
word.

If the penitent sinner were automatically free, why does Christ
tell His disciples that they should preach forgiveness to repenting
sinners, assuring them that whose soever sins they remit they are
remitted to them? These words of Christ are entirely super-
fluous and misleading if He does not mean that pardon is to be
declared to the penitent sinner, and that he is free when this is
done—not before. The Bible never teaches that a penitent sinner
is automatically free; it says that his sins are forgiven when one
of the disciples of Jesus declares them forgiven, and when he
believes it. The example of David shows this. He says: "I acknowledged my sin unto thee, and mine iniquity have I not hid: I
said, I will confess my transgressions unto the Lord; and thou
forgavest the iniquity of my sin." [93] As we read in the twelfth
chapter of Second Samuel, David confessed his sins to the Lord
in the presence of Nathan, and the Lord forgave him the iniquity
of his sin through the word of Nathan, when this prophet declared to him, "The Lord also hath put away thy sin; thou shalt
not die." The Bible truly promises forgiveness to the person who
repents of his sins and confesses them, but it is presumption to

pass by or reject the agency by which God forgives, namely, the Gospel declared by one of his servants—just as it would be presumption if the criminal in prison, after reading news of the pardon granted to him, should rush out, without waiting for an official to come and declare it to him and lead him out, or even without asking a warden about it. In my view, the necessity of hearing the Gospel of forgiveness from one of the servants of God is not an annoying and legalistic order. I feel it is a privilege, a good gift of God, that I can hear such a declaration and assurance to myself, and receive it as a word coming from the very heart of God. Respect for the majesty of God and Christ requires that we conscientiously follow His orders in the Scriptures. Then we may be sure that we have not gone to our own ways.

Your thought that when a man complies to the God-prescribed prerequisites he is automatically free implies a grave danger of self-righteousness. The sinner is led to think: When I comply, when I fulfill the conditions, then I am automatically free. A lot of emphasis is laid on what he does in the way of an adequate fulfillment of the prerequisites. This is hardly the way of the Gospel. The Gospel way is this: the sinner is not told to fulfill the prerequisites; rather, when he is in despair because of his sins, the Gospel of a fully sufficient redemption and forgiveness of sins in the blood of Christ is proclaimed to him. He simply receives this promise, depending on it in faith. I am afraid that if I were first to fulfill the prerequisites and then believe that I am automatically free, I could never believe. I would remain endeavoring to comply to the prerequisites—and probably would never be able.

When I speak of absolution, or declaration of the forgiveness of sins to a penitent sinner—whether he is a sinner about to be converted or a sin-burdened Christian—I do not only mean the personal absolution, or application of the Gospel promise to a person individually. I also mean the public proclamation of the Gospel in sermons. The pardon of the heavenly King is declared in public preaching too, and, of course, in baptism. You do not believe that in baptism sins are forgiven, just as you do not believe that sins are forgiven through the proclamation of the Gospel. We believe both, since the Bible so teaches. In fact, baptism is one form of using the Christ-given power to remit sins; personal absolution is the second form; preaching of forgiveness in public sermons is the third form; and to Christians the assurance of forgiveness in Christ's blood is also given in the

Lord's Supper. To all of these forms of Gospel administration apply the words of Christ: "Whose soever sins ye remit, they are remitted unto them."

John: What you say seems to be worth consideration. I will ponder this matter and pray that the Lord open my understanding to see His will and ways, and to follow them.

Martin: May the Lord bless you in that purpose of your heart and lead you to the knowledge and obedience of His truth.

NOTES

II. The Meaning and Blessing of Baptism

1. Augustus Hopkins Strong, *Systematic Theology* (5th ed., revised and enlarged; New York: Armstrong and Son, 1896), pp. 527-531, 535, 538. Edward T. Hiscox, *The New Directory for Baptist Churches* (Philadelphia: American Baptist Publication Society, 1894), pp. 123-127, 389, 482. William L. Pettingill, "The Evils of Infant Baptism." Reprinted in Dr. J. Oliver Buswell's booklet *Both Sides of the Baptism Question,* p. 2.
2. On the Campbellites, see Strong, *op. cit.,* p. 534; Buswell, *op. cit.,* p. 9; and the Schaff-Herzog *Encyclopedia of Religious Knowledge.*
3. Matt. 28:19-20.
4. Acts 2:36ff.
5. H. A. Ironside, *Baptism: What Saith the Scripture* (3d ed., 1930), p. 19.
6. Luke 24:27.
7. Acts 22:16.
8. Acts 9:17.
9. Ironside, *op. cit.,* pp. 20, 28f.
10. Such as Dr. Ironside, for instance.
11. Ironside, *op. cit.,* p. 45.
12. The Authorized Version: ". . . sanctify and cleanse it with the washing of water by the word . . ."
13. Eph. 5:25-26.
14. 1 Pet. 3:21. Thus the A. V. The R. V. has: ". . . which also after a true likeness (or, in the antitype) doth now save you, even baptism, not the putting away of the filth of the flesh, but the interrogation (or, inquiry) of a good conscience toward God . . ."
15. Ironside, *op. cit.,* p. 26.
16. Luther, *On the Lord's Supper. Confession,* 1528, Weimar ed., vol. 26, p. 506.
17. Acts 8:36-38.
18. Mark 16:16.
19. *Ibid.*
20. Ironside, *op. cit.,* pp. 5, 30.
21. Ironside, *op. cit.,* p. 22.

22. James 1:18; I Pet. 1:23-25.
23. Ironside, *op. cit.*, pp. 10f.
24. John 15:3.
25. Luke 7:30.
26. Strong, *op. cit.*, pp. 534, 536.
27. John 1:12.
28. Gal. 4:3-6.
29. John 15:3.
30. John 13:10-11.
31. Acts 8:1-17.
32. Acts 10:43-48.
33. Matt. 7:21-23.
34. Rom. 8:9.
35. Matt. 25:1-12.
36. 2 Tim. 3:5.
37. Luke 13:24-28.
38. John 10:27-28.
39. 1 Pet. 1:23.
40. James 1:18.
41. 1 Cor. 4:15.
42. John 1:12; 3:5, 6, 8. Gal. 4:29. 1 John 2:29; 3:9; 4:7; 5:1, 4, 18.
43. 1 Cor. 1:17.
44. Rom. 1:17.
45. Strong, *op. cit.*, pp. 299f., 449ff.
46. John 3:5-7, 3, 5.
47. Rom. 10:17.
48. John Calvin, *Institutes of the Christian Religion*, trans. John Allen (7th Am. ed., Philadelphia: Presbyterian Board of Christian Education), II, p. 596.
49. The Weimar edition of Luther's works: vol. 12, p. 590; vol. 27, p. 190; vol. 47, pp. 40, 45.
50. Luther, *Unterricht der Visitatoren*, 1528, Weimar ed., vol. 26, pp. 202f.
51. Calvin, *Institutes, op. cit.*, pp. 620-622, says to the point: "It is necessary for us to be engrafted into Him, that we may be rescued from the bondage of death. But how, it is inquired, are infants regenerated, who have no knowledge either of good or evil? We reply, that the work of God is not yet without existence because it is not observed or understood by us . . . I would beg them to inform me, what danger can result from our affirming that they already receive some portion of that grace, of which they will ere long enjoy the full abundance . . . As the Lord, therefore, will illuminate them [infants who are baptized and die young] with the full splendor of His countenance in heaven, why may He not also, if such be His pleasure, irradiate them with some faint rays of it in the present life; . . . Not that I would hastily affirm them to be endued with the same faith which we experience in ourselves, or at all to possess a similar knowledge of faith."
52. Pettingill, *op. cit.*, p. 2.

53. Strong, *op. cit.*, pp. 537ff.
54. Acts 2:39.
55. Calvin, *Institutes*, book IV, ch. XVI, sec. xv, *op. cit.*, pp. 617f.
56. John 10:27-29.
57. John 6:39-40.
58. Rom. 8:38-39.
59. Rom. 8:29-30.
60. 1 Cor. 1:8-9.
61. 1 Pet. 1:5.
62. 1 John 3:2.
63. Matt. 7:21-23.
64. New York: Loizeaux Brothers, 1924.
65. Moline, Ill.; Strombeck Agency, Inc., 1936.
66. John 15:6.
67. Strombeck, *op. cit.*, p. 158.
68. Matt. 10:22; 24:13. Mark 13:13.
69. Strombeck, *op. cit.*, p. 145.
70. Gal. 3:28.
71. Tim. 4:1.
72. 1 Pet. 2:3.
73. Heb. 10:29.
74. Luke 15.
75. Eph. 1:10.
76. Gal. 5:42.
77. 1 Cor. 9:27.
78. Mark 1:15.
79. Luke 24:47.
80. Ps. 14:1.
81. John 20:21-23.
82. Matt. 16:19.
83. Matt. 18:18.
84. Luke 10:16.
85. 2 Cor. 5:20.
86. John 14:12.
87. Matt. 9:2.
88. Eph. 1:7. 1 John 1:7.
89. Heb. 10:22.
90. Heb. 12:24.
91. 1 Pet. 1:2.
92. Matt. 15:6.
93. Ps. 32:5.

III. The Testimony of History

John: We have discussed a question which does not directly belong to our actual topic. Let's turn back to baptism. As I see it, the history of the Christian Church plainly shows that infant baptism is a late invention of the Catholic Church.

Martin: A while ago we discussed the teachings of Jesus on baptism in the context of the historical situation during His public ministry. We saw that both this context and the direct teachings of our Lord point in the direction of infant baptism. Let us now turn to the testimony of church history after the Apostolic Age.

1. THE ANCIENT CHURCH

John: Tertullian is the first writer who mentions infant baptism in history, and he opposes it, although Neander supposes that the much disputed passage of Irenaeus has reference to this custom, a little earlier than Tertullian's mention of it. Tertullian opposed infant baptism at the close of the second century, or about A.D. 200. His opposition proves two things: first, that it was in occasional use, at least; second, that it was of recent origin and not generally prevalent. For it must have been in use to be discussed and opposed, and had it been long prevalent it would have been earlier mentioned.

Church historians who have studied the history of the post-Apostolic Age show that infant baptism was unknown until the first part of the third century after Christ. Had it existed earlier, some trace of, or allusion to, it would have been discovered.

It should be added that when the baptism of children did begin to be practiced, it was not the baptism of unconscious infants at all, but, as Bunsen says, of "little growing children, from six to ten years old." He declares that Tertullian, in his opposition to infant baptism, does not say a word about newborn babes.

Cyprian, an African bishop, at the close of the third century urged the baptism of infants proper, because of the regenerating efficacy which the ordinance was supposed to exert. He and his associates were the first to take this ground. It was believed that

81

baptism conveyed saving grace to the soul. Anxious parents therefore desired their dying children to receive baptism, and thus through "washing in the laver of regeneration" be secured against the perils of perdition. Such was one of the errors of a superstitious age. Hence arose infant baptism, as one of the many perversions which early corrupted the doctrines and ordinances of Christianity.[1]

Martin: You have an inconsistency in what you stated. First, you said that Tertullian opposed infant baptism at the close of the *second* century, and that it must have then been in use for some time. But a little later you said that there is no allusion to infant baptism before the first part of the *third* century, and that it was unknown before that. Did you forget what you stated before?

John: You are right. I was inconsistent. I admit that infant baptism was in use, at least to some extent, in the second half of the second century.

Martin: You also seem to have forgotten what you admitted a while ago, namely, that belief in the grace-conveying efficacy of baptism is no superstition of a later time but a clear and incontestable teaching of the New Testament. You can hardly mean that some teachings of the New Testament are superstitious?

John: Certainly not. But isn't it a historical fact that infant baptism was unknown until the second half of the second century, or at least that it is not mentioned before that time in the writings of the post-Apostolic Age?

Martin: Let us see what Irenaeus says in the statement that you called "much disputed." This teacher of the church was born in A.D. 140 or about forty years after the death of the apostle John. In his youth he was a disciple of Polycarp, bishop of Smyrna, who in turn had been a disciple of John. Irenaeus writes: "Christ came to save all people through Himself, I say all who through Him are born again to God, nursing babes, small children, children, young people, and older people; therefore He passed through all the different ages, becoming a nursing infant for the sake of nursing infants . . ."[2]

John: Irenaeus does not mention baptism at all, and probably he only speaks of Christ as the Savior of all men in general.

Martin: He says that Christ saves those who are through Him *born to God*. Then he goes on to explain that even nursing babes are born to God through Christ. How can a nursing babe be born to God except through baptism?

John: True, that seems to be the only possible conclusion.

Martin: Irenaeus says in the same book that baptism is "a baptism of new birth to God." [3] These words show that he means baptism when he speaks of the new birth. This way of speaking originated with Christ Himself—or already in the Synagogue—and it was quite common in the second century. Justin the Martyr, who was born in the first years of the second century and suffered a martyr's death in A.D. 165, writes: "Then we lead them to a place where there is water and give them a new birth in the same manner as we were born again, for they are washed in water in the name of God, the Father and ruler of all, and Jesus Christ, our Redeemer, and the Holy Ghost." [4]

Justin also wrote that many men and women had "been disciples already as children." Many of these men and women who had become disciples already as children must have been baptized in the apostolic age (if they were older than Justin), or soon after it (if they were of his age), for they became disciples of Christ in baptism. Justin does not, however, state how old these children were at the time of their baptism. Irenaeus says that even nursing babes were born again (by baptism). These words of Justin and Irenaeus imply that both in the first and second part of the second century the Church believed in baptismal regeneration and practiced baptism of children.

One of the best known examples of infant baptism in the second half of the second century is Origen, the greatest theologian of the Ancient Church. He was born in A.D. 185 or 186 and was baptized in his infancy. He writes: "Baptism is, according to the usages of the Church, given also to infants." [5] "The Church has received from the apostles the tradition to give baptism even to infants. For those who were entrusted with the divine mysteries knew that all men have the natural pollution of sin, which must be washed away through water and the Spirit. No man is free from the defilement of sin, even if he is one day old. Since the inborn uncleanness is washed away through baptism, little children also come to be baptized. For unless one is born of water and the Spirit he cannot enter into the kingdom of God." [6]

Some Baptists say that Origen doesn't speak of the baptism of infants but of older children. That is not true, for he speaks of *one-day-old* infants, and explains that infant baptism is a tradition received from the apostles.

Origen lived so close to the Apostolic Age that only one man's lifetime had passed between Apostle John's death and Origen's birth and baptism. You present-day Baptists live almost 1800 years after. Is it reasonable to think that you are in a better position to know what is an apostolic tradition than a man who lived less than a hundred years after the Apostolic Age?

Bishop Cyprian, a contemporary of Origen, declared that they were mistaken who held that infants should not be baptized before the eighth day after their birth.[7] In A.D. 253 the Church Council of Carthage followed this view of Cyprian in its decision on infant baptism. There was no doubt about infant baptism itself.

Let us now return to Tertullian, who was about half a century younger than Origen and Cyprian. In his famous statement against infant baptism he writes: "According to the circumstances and disposition, and even age, of each individual, the delay of baptism is preferable, principally, however, in the case of little children. For why is it necessary . . . that sponsors likewise should be thrust into danger—who both themselves, by reason of mortality, may fail to fulfill their promises, and may be disappointed by the development of an evil disposition in those for whom they stood . . . Why should little babes, the innocent ones, haste to the forgiveness of sins? . . . Unmarried people also have as much reason to postpone baptism because they are apt to be tempted, virgins because of their maturity and widows because of their loneliness, until they have either married or have become so strong that they are able to practice continence. If one really understands the value of baptism, he is more afraid of receiving it than of postponing it."[8]

You said a while ago, referring to Bunsen, that Tertullian in his opposition to infant baptism does not say a word about new-born infants.[9] That is not true, for Tertullian speaks of "little babes, the innocent ones," who obviously are newly born infants, in whom the evil tendencies of human flesh have not yet developed. Or do you, brother John, think that five-to-ten-year-old children can be called "little babes, the innocent ones," in whom no evil tendencies have developed?

John: Of course not. Children of that age are no longer innocent; neither can they be called little babes.

Martin: Then you admit that Tertullian speaks of infant baptism. Let's see what are his reasons in opposing it. He does not say that infant baptism is wrong, or that it is not of apostolic origin. He only thinks that it is preferable to postpone baptism because the sponsors may fail, because of death, to fulfill their promises, or because evil tendencies may develop in the baptized children when they grow up. For similar reasons unmarried young people and widows should postpone their baptism. Would you accept such reasons for postponing baptism?

John: No, certainly not. In our time hardly anyone would even think of such reasons.

Martin: We conclude that Tertullian opposed infant baptism for some reasons of expediency, not because of principle, and his reasons cannot be regarded as valid and acceptable. His words that little babes *(parvuli)* "haste" to the forgiveness of sins seem to indicate that infants were taken to baptism as early as possible. In his time some Christians (particularly the Montanists) held the view that in baptism all sins were forgiven and washed away, but sins after baptism were almost unforgivable. Tertullian was one of those who held this erroneous notion, and that was the reason why he recommended its postponement.

Our study of the testimony of the history of the post-Apostolic Church has led us to the result that infant baptism was practiced in the first half of the second century, that is, during the fifty years after the death of the apostle John, and that it was held to be a tradition received from the apostles. Tertullian was the only one who opposed it, and even his opposition was based on entirely wrong premises.

Antipedobaptists often say that infant baptism has always gone hand-in-hand with state churches.[10] That assertion is repeated even in America, which has no state churches, at least not in the United States and Canada.

In Europe many of the churches that practice infant baptism have never been state churches. Or have the Lutheran churches of Hungary, the Balkan states, Austria, Poland, Russia, France, and Holland, or the Reformed churches of the same countries and England ever been state churches?

John: I know that they have never been state churches.

Martin: They have been free churches which have frequently suffered persecution. Martyrdom is no "privilege" of antipedo-baptists. An unprejudiced study of church history shows that usually there has been no direct or indirect connection between infant baptism and state churches. These churches use infant baptism simply because they regard it as Biblical.

2. THE MIDDLE AGES

John: Doctor Pettingill says: "At all time, from the beginning of the church age, God has always had a remnant remaining faithful to Him. They have never consented to the union of church and state, or to baptismal regeneration, or to infant baptism. . . . They bore nicknames, depending sometimes upon a leader's name, or the name of their locality. They were Montanists, Novatians, Paulicians, Arnoldists, Henricians, Petro-Brussians, Waldenses, Peterines, Albigenses, Stundists, and others; but their generic name was Anabaptists, meaning rebaptizers, for they ignored infant baptism, and rebaptized those who had been saved through personal faith. They also had a generic name for themselves; they called themselves Antipedobaptists, meaning opponents of infant baptism." 11

Doesn't this fact, pointed out by Doctor Pettingill, show that Baptism has existed from the Apostolic times on?

Martin: Do you know these groups from church history?

John: Except for this statement of Doctor Pettingill's, I have only read what Hiscox says on the matter.12

Martin: Let's see what church history says of these groups. Montanists are the first group mentioned by Doctor Pettingill. Doctor Thomas Armitage declares in his large work *History of the Baptists* 13 that the Montanists sprang from Montanus, a native of Phrygia, in Asia Minor. The movement aimed at restoring the Church to its original spirituality and purity. The aim was good, but in trying to accomplish their end they went too far and fell into errors. They claimed that they were as directly under the special inspiration of the Holy Spirit as were the apostles, and that Montanus was the Holy Spirit Himself. They became thoroughly legal in their zeal for consecration, excluded themselves from society, and were harsh in their treatment of weak and erring Christians. Sin after baptism was regarded by them as almost unpardonable; second marriages were regarded as wicked in the extreme; and matter itself was held to be unmixed evil.

Tertullian joined the Montanists and shared their view of sins after baptism. That was the reason why he opposed infant baptism, as well as the baptism of unmarried virgins and widows. Otherwise, there was no dispute on baptism between the Montanists and the Church Universal, Doctor Armitage says. Both of them believed that sins were forgiven in baptism, and both of them regarded baptism as a washing of regeneration. Both of them also used infant baptism, although there was more tendency among the Montanists to postpone it to a later age, as the example of Tertullian shows. As I pointed out, this was due to the Montanist view that sins after baptism were almost unpardonable. The Church Universal, or the Catholic Church—not the Roman

Catholic, which did not exist as yet—was more merciful in its treatment of weak and erring Christians, and of those who fell into apostasy in persecutions.

Now, brother John, can you tell me in what sense were the Montanists antipedobaptists? I repeat, there was no controversy on baptism between them and the Church at large, and in things on which there was controversy, the antipedobaptists of our time do not accept the Montanistic conception but agree with the Ancient Catholic Church.

John: It seems to me that the Montanists are not akin to the antipedobaptists in any other sense than in their zeal for the purity of the Church.

Martin: But in the principles to be followed in caring for the purity and spirituality of the Church the antipedobaptists follow the principles of the Ancient Catholic Church. We are therefore much closer to historical truth when we say that the Montanists cannot be regarded in any special sense as forerunners of the baptistic principles. Even their view that it is preferable to baptize people in mature age than in infancy has little to do with the modern baptistic principles; quite to the contrary, it was based on their belief in the saving efficacy of baptism, and on their conception that sins after baptism were almost unpardonable; and both of these beliefs are in conflict with present-day baptistic teaching.

The Novatians were "Puritans" who arose about a century later than the Montanists, taking their name from Novatian, a Roman Christian who was their first notable leader. Novatian was sick when he was baptized, and it was done by pouring water on him. Such an emergency form of baptism was regarded as doubtful by some strict immersionists, particularly when it came to ordaining such a person for ministry. Cornelius, a rival of Novatian in Rome, used this fact against him when he wanted to become a presbyter and bishop. Another controversial issue was that Novatian opposed the restoration of the "lapsed" into the Church, while Cornelius favored their reception after due repentance. When Cornelius was elected bishop by the majority in A.D. 251, Novatian let the minority elect him also a bishop, and so he became the leader of a strict party which excluded permanently from their church fallen Christians, and also rebaptized all who joined them from the Catholic Church.

John: The Novatians represented, then, a baptistic principle.

Martin: Don't be too rash in your conclusions. The Novatians, like the Church in general, believed in salvation through bap-

tism. The antipedobaptists of our time (with the exception of
the Campbellites) do not believe in it. The Novatians did not
rebaptize the Catholics because they had been baptized before
conversion, but simply because they came from a Church which
they regarded as corrupt, since it received "lapsed" or fallen
people who repented and wanted to return to the Church. It
seems to me that the antipedobaptists of our time follow at this
point the principles of the Church Universal of the fourth century, not the principles of the Novatians. If there were Novatians
in our time, we may be sure that they would denounce practically
all the antipedobaptists as corrupt because they receive fallen
Christians back into the Church when they repent. The Novatians would reimmerse all the Baptists, Pentecostals, and such
others who would join them, as coming from corrupt churches.
Besides, as Doctor Armitage says, no controversy existed between
the Church Universal and the Novatians on baptism itself, and
there was no discussion on infant baptism between them. Thus
I do not see any reason at all why some antipedobaptists regard
the Novatians as representatives of their principles.

   Of the Paulicians, Doctor Armitage tells that they were a group
that arose in Armenia about A.D. 660, and probably got their
name from the Apostle Paul, whom they greatly admired. They
were not Baptists, for they rejected all external sacraments, using
no baptism at all. The words of the Gospel were, in their judgment, the only baptism and communion for the faithful. They
believed in a baptism known as the Consolamentum or baptism
of the Spirit, which they administered by laying a copy of the
Gospels on the head of the candidate, accompanied with prayer.
As to the Supper, they fed on Christ only by faith in the heart,
regarding this as the spirit of the institution. In a word, on the
ordinances they were related to the Quakers, and not to the antipedobaptists. The Paulicians were Reformed Manicheans, who
rejected many of the doctrines of this sect, which was a mixture
of Christianity and the pagan religion of the Persians. They held,
however, some of the tenets of the Gnostics, and were filled with
all kinds of speculations as to the nature of God, the origin of
matter, its relations to moral and physical evil, and so were poor
specimens of Christians anyway, when measured after the full
order of the Gospel, as Doctor Armitage says.[14] Now, brother
John, in what sense are the Paulicians to be regarded as representatives of the baptistic principles?

   John: I do not see any particular similarity between them and
the followers of baptistic principles in our time. I wonder why

Doctor Pettingill mentions them among the ancient representatives of baptistic principles.

Martin: I also wonder. Even the fact that they were persecuted
is no peculiarity of theirs, for the Church Universal was also
persecuted until the first part of the fourth century, and the
Lutheran and Reformed pedobaptists have at times been persecuted as much as any Baptists.

The Petro-Brussians, or Petrobrusians, were followers of Peter
of Bruis in the twelfth century. They were a part of the movement called Cathari, but rejected many of the tenets of the actual
Cathari. They abandoned infant baptism and insisted on immersion of all believers in Christ. Peter of Bruis began his
reformation movement in A.D. 1104. He rejected the Catholic doctrine of transubstantiation and regarded the Lord's Supper as a
merely historical and memorial act. He held the Church to be
made up of a regenerated people only, counted the bishops and
priests, as he knew them, mere frauds, rejected the adoration of
images, prayers for the dead, and the doctrine of baptismal regeneration.[15] The Petrobrusians were thus in their doctrine and
practice true Medieval Baptists. Arnold of Brescia, from whom
the Arnoldists received their name, was in 1139 condemned by
the Lateran Council for rejecting infant baptism. He was possibly at this point a follower of Peter of Bruis. Arnold has become
famous for the establishment of a republic in Rome, which,
however, came to its end when Frederick Barbarossa conquered
the city, and Arnold himself was hanged in 1155.[16]

The Henricians were followers of Henry of Lausanne, an
itinerant preacher who lived about the same time as Arnold of
Brescia and Bernard of Clairvaux. He remained true to the
Catholic doctrine, which is seen from the fact that, although he
was taken before the Council of Pisa, he was not condemned as a
heretic. Thus he has nothing to do with the history of Baptism.
Because of this fact, Armitage does not mention the Henricians
at all.

The Waldensians are named after Peter Waldo, a rich mer-
chant of Lyons. In 1160 he consecrated himself to Christ, began
to preach, had the Gospels translated into the language of the
common people, and became a leader of a movement that spread
in southern France, northern Italy, and elsewhere. They did not
reject the doctrine of the Church, and therefore they were accused
only of being "schismatics," because they established a new apos-
tolate, and usurped the office of preaching without papal authority. They were excommunicated in 1183-84. After that they

gradually became critical of some doctrines of the Church of Rome on the basis of the teachings of the Scriptures, which they diligently studied. In general they did not oppose infant baptism. Doctor Armitage writes: "If they opposed infant baptism it is unaccountable that their literature, running through four centuries, gives no formal argument against it, and no accompanying demand for the baptism of believers only." Neither did they defend infant baptism.[17] The reason must be that there was no dissension on baptism between them and the Catholic Church. There were, however, possibly some individual Waldensians who accepted the view of the Peterbrusians, but they were exceptions. This is also seen from the fact that the bulk of the Waldensians joined the Protestant pedobaptists at the time of the Reformation, having with them no dissension on baptism. Thus, the Waldensians were not forerunners of Baptism, but rather of pedobaptist Protestants.

The Albigenses arose in southern France early in the eleventh century, taking their name from the city of Albi, the center of the Albigenses district. They rejected the Romish Church, and esteemed the New Testament above all its traditions and ceremonies. The Catholic Church organized crusades against them, and their district was utterly destroyed and the people slaughtered. Since there were many sects of the Cathari, among whom the Albigenses were counted, it is hard to know their doctrines. It is known that they did not take oaths, and did not believe in baptismal regeneration. They were ascetic, and exalted celibacy. Only certain minor groups of the Cathari rejected infant baptism.[18]

The Paterenes or Patarenes were a reform party at Milan in the eleventh century, directed against the worldly behavior of the clergy and the so-called royal investiture. The clergy was compelled to celibacy, and the property of the refractory clergy was plundered. The Patarenes were thoroughly Roman Catholic in doctrine and never questioned infant baptism.[19] It is inconceivable to me why Doctor Pettingill mentions this Catholic riotous party, zealous for the celibacy of the clergy, among the forerunners and representatives of baptistic principles. In reality it has nothing to do with the history of Baptism. Doctor Armitage does not mention them at all. Neither does he mention the Stundists, an evangelical revival movement in southern Russia, which received its inspiration from German Lutheran immigrants. It was led by a layman, Ratusny, in the 1860's, and came soon into a close contact with Baptism. Stundism was not originally a Baptist movement, and as far as it has been influenced by Baptism, its history belongs to the modern history of Baptism.

The result of our study is that most of the groups mentioned by Doctor Pettingill cannot be called Anabaptists, and still less have they used this name of themselves, as Doctor Pettingill asserts. Most of them have nothing to do with the history of Baptism.[20]

A historical fact is that the baptistic view of baptism is not found in the Bible; neither is it found in the history of the Church for more than a millennium after the birth of the Church. No group held the baptistic principles in the Christian Church until the appearance of the Petrobrusians. Thus the history of Baptism begins about 1104, and all attempts to trace it farther back than that have failed, or have been based on a falsification of facts. In the actual sense of the word, the history of the baptistic movement begins in 1525 in the form of the Reformation-period Anabaptists. According to the study of Harold S. Bender, who belongs to the Mennonites, the direct spiritual descendents of the Anabaptists, the birthday of the Anabaptist movement was January 21, 1525, in the city of Zurich, Switzerland. Then a number of men assembled privately for prayer and meditation, and a certain George Blaurock, a former cleric of Grisonia, asked the leader of the group, Conrad Grebel, to seal his decision for a new and committed life by baptizing him upon confession of faith. This Grebel did. Then he himself was baptized by Blaurock, and after that the other members of this small circle were also baptized. It was a solemn and spontaneous act in which no known outside influences seem to have been instrumental.[21] It was a new start, without any connection with the medieval Petrobrusians and other baptists. As I already pointed out, in our time the Mennonites and some other groups are descendants of the sixteenth century Anabaptists. The baptistic movement of the English-speaking world started in the 1590's among the followers of Henry Barrow. A certain person had himself rebaptized, and than baptized others. This was another new start, without a direct historical connection with the Anabaptists. Thus both in doctrine and practice the baptistic view is a relatively late unbiblical error. When the Baptist writers claim that "Baptists have an unbroken line of churches since Christ," and that even during the Middle Ages (A.D. 500-1520) there has been "a continual line of churches called Ana-Baptists,"[22] they speak historical untruths.

John: I cannot deny that your hard judgment is largely justified. I am not able to show any group in the Church that has really represented the baptistic view until the Petrobrusians. But we haven't discussed as yet the mode of baptism. I think the picture is different when we turn to that question. If you will bear with me, I will explain our doctrine in that respect.

NOTES

III. The Testimony of History

1. Edward T. Hiscox, *The New Directory for Baptist Churches* (Philadelphia: American Baptist Publication Society, 1894), pp. 477ff.
2. Iranaeus, *Adversus haereses*, II, 22.
3. *Ibid.*, I, 18.
4. Justin, *Apology.*
5. Origen, "Eighth Homily on Lev. 3"; in Migne, *Patrologia Graeca*, XIV, 496.
6. Origen, "Commentary on Romans," V. 9; Migne, *op. cit.*, 1047.
7. Cyprian, Epistle 58, Ante-Nicene Fathers, V, 353f.
8. Tertullian, *De baptismo*, 18.
9. According to Hiscox, *op. cit.*, p. 479.
10. Augustus Hopkins Strong, *Systematic Theology* (5th ed. revised and enlarged; New York: Armstrong and Son, 1896), p. 536.
11. William L. Pettingill, "The Evils of Infant Baptism." Reprinted in Dr. J. Oliver Buswell's booklet *Both Sides of the Baptism Question*, p. 3.
12. Hiscox, *op. cit.*, pp. 495ff.
13. New York: Bryan, Taylor and Co., 1887. Dr. Armitage was pastor of the Fifth Avenue Baptist Church in New York City. He deals with Montanism on pp. 174-177.
14. Armitage, *op. cit.*, pp. 234ff.
15. *Ibid.*, pp. 284ff.
16. *Ibid.*, pp. 292f.
17. *Ibid.*, pp. 295-302.
18. *Ibid.*, pp. 278ff.
19. Schaff-Herzog, *New Encyclopedia of Religious Knowledge.*
20. Dr. Pettingill explains in his article "The Evils of Infant Baptism" that "in church history their is no record of infant baptism until the year 370." We have shown how another Baptist, Hiscox, admits that Tertullian's opposition to infant baptism toward the end of the second century shows that it had then been in use for some time. Dr. Pettingill also declares that "in the year 416 infant baptism was made compulsory throughout the Roman empire by law." Church history knows nothing of such an event. The whole thing is an invention of Dr. Pettingill, who has much zeal against infant baptism, but does not seem to care for

historical truth. Dr. J. Oliver Buswell sent to *The Voice*, in which Pettingill's article was published, an article in which he refuted Pettingill's errors, but *The Voice* (official organ of the Independent Fundamental Churches of America) refused to publish it. Dr. Buswell published both Pettingill's article and his own in *The Bible Today*. They are available as a reprint from Shelton College, New York.

21. H. S. Bender, *Conrad Grebel, c.* 1498-1525, *the Founder of the Swiss Brethren, Sometimes Called Anabaptists* (Goshen, Indiana: The Mennonite Historical Society, 1950).

22. J. M. Carrol, *"The Trail of Blood"* (Lexington, Ky.: Ashland Avenue Baptist Church, 1931). Chart at the end of the booklet.

IV. The Mode of Baptism

John: The mode of baptism is immersion and immersion only, for the command to baptize is a command to immerse, since the word *baptizein* means "to dip in or under water," in Latin *immergere*. Every passage in the New Testament where the word occurs either requires or allows the meaning "immerse." That is also seen from the circumstances attending the administration of baptism. In the first chapter of Mark, tenth verse, we read that Jesus "came out of the water," and John, third chapter, twenty-third verse, tells us that there was much water in the place where John was baptizing. Likewise, in the narrative of the conversion of the Ethiopian eunuch we are told that Philip and the eunuch "went down into the water," and then "came up out of the water."

Moreover, the mode of baptism is also clear from the figurative allusions to the ordinance, for example, in Romans, sixth chapter, fourth verse, where Paul says that baptism means burial and resurrection with Christ. Only immersion can depict and symbolize such a burial and resurrection.

Church history shows that immersion was a universal custom in the Christian Church for about a millennium after its birth.[1] You are probably acquainted with the first detailed instruction concerning the mode of baptism, contained in the *Teaching of the Lord through the Twelve Apostles*, also called *Didache*, written in the early part of the second century. This booklet shows the baptismal practice of the Ancient Church. We read there:

"Concerning baptism, thus baptize ye: Having first said all these things, baptize into the name of the Father, and the Son, and of the Holy Spirit, in living water. But if thou have not living water, baptize in other water; and if thou canst not in cold, in warm. But if thou have not either, pour out water three times upon the head in the name of the Father, and the Son, and the Holy Ghost."[2]

According to this instruction, pouring was used in cases of emergency, when immersion could not be used. Immersion in a living or running water was the ordinary and preferable mode of baptism. This was the rule for about a thousand years. Aspersion or sprinkling and pouring is a papal corruption accepted by most Protestants.

Martin: All that you say is well known to me. I have carefully studied what Strong, Hiscox and many other Baptist, Pentecostal and Adventist writers say on the matter. I also know that Luther recommended immersion as the proper mode of baptism. In fact, Doctor Strong quotes his statement: Baptism is "a sign both of death and resurrection. Being moved by this reason, I would have those that are baptized to be altogether dipped into the water, as the word means and the mystery signifies." [3]

I know two similar statements given by Luther. In his *Treatise on Baptism*, published in 1519, he says: "Baptism is called in the Greek language *baptismos*, in Latin *mersio*, which means to plunge something entirely into the water, so that the water closes over it. And although in many places it is the custom no longer to thrust and plunge children into the font of baptism, but only to pour the baptismal water upon them out of the font, nevertheless the former is what should be done." [4]

And he says again: "It would be better that, according to the meaning of the word *baptize*, the child, or whoever is baptized, should be immersed into water and then lifted up. For there is no doubt that the German *Taufe* (baptism) is derived from the word *tief* (deep), as the person who is baptized is dipped into water. The significance of baptism also requires it, for it means that the old man and the sinful nature, which is of flesh and blood, must be wholly drowned by the grace of God." [5]

Calvin says about the same thing: "The very word *baptize* . . . signifies to immerse; and it is certain that immersion was the practice of the ancient Church." [6]

John: Why, then, didn't Luther and Calvin reintroduce immersion?

Martin: That's what I also have wondered. They had a long struggle with the Anabaptists of their time, and the Anabaptists used immersion. Luther and Calvin rejected the Anabaptist view of baptism because they regarded it as unbiblical, and obviously they were right in their view at this point. They acknowledged the mode of baptism used by the Anabaptists as correct and recommended its use. But they did not regard immersion as essential. In their view, the significance and efficacy of baptism did not depend on its outward mode, since the external act was only a seal to the promise of the Gospel. The efficacy of baptism was in the word of God and faith, not in the outward mode of it. Therefore, although they recommended immersion, they did not regard the matter important enough to make an effort to reintroduce it into practice.

John: The reformers admitted that the word "baptize" means "to immerse." Why, then, do many pedobaptists defend the view that it does not necessarily mean immersion? Isn't that dishonesty and disregard of historical fact?

Martin: Not quite. When we study the use of the word *baptizein* (or *baptein,* from which the former is a frequentative derivative) in the Greek translation of the Old Testament, known as Septuagint (LXX), which was the Bible of most early Christians, and which is usually quoted in the Greek New Testament, we see that it does not always mean "to immerse." In the book of Ecclesiasticus (Sirach), thirty-fourth chapter, thirtieth verse, we read: "He who baptizes himself from the dead *(baptizomenos apo nekrou),* and touches it again, what benefit does he have from his washing?" According to the nineteenth chapter of Numbers, eighteenth and nineteenth verses, cleansing after touching a dead corpse was done by sprinkling and not by immersion. In the just quoted passage of Ecclesiasticus, the word *baptizein* must therefore mean ceremonial cleansing by sprinkling. In the fourteenth chapter of Leviticus, sixth verse, we read: "As for the living bird, he shall take it, and the cedar wood, and the scarlet, and the hyssop, and shall dip *(bapsei)* them and the living bird in the blood of the bird . . ." There was obviously not enough blood to immerse these objects in. The word *baptein* must have here a meaning equivalent to the secondary meaning of the English "dip": "To put or sink slightly or partially into a liquid."

In Daniel, fourth chapter, thirty-third verse, we read: "And he (Nebuchadnezzar) was driven from men, and his body was wet *(ebaphe,* from *baptein)* with the dew of heaven." The meaning of *baptein* is here about the same as in the previous usage. In the tenth chapter of First Corinthians, Paul speaks figuratively of the baptism of the Israelites unto Moses in the cloud and the sea. It was no immersion, for the cloud was above the Tabernacle or before the people, and never surrounded them; and in the sea the Israelites walked on dry ground, the waters being on both sides of them. Probably only their feet were moistened by the somewhat wet bottom of the sea. In Mark, seventh chapter, fourth verse, some manuscripts have *rhantisontai* (sprinkled themselves), while others have *baptisontai* (baptized themselves), which shows that the words meaning "sprinkling" and "baptizing" were sometimes used interchangeably.

These examples of the use of the words *baptein* and *baptizein* show that they do not always mean "to immerse," as those who hold the baptistic doctrine maintain. Like the English word "dip," these words can mean total immersion, partial immersion, or slight immersion, and sometimes even sprinkling. The word *baptizein* is used of various kinds of ceremonial or sacred cleansings by means of water, blood, or other agent. We should also remember that the word "baptism" is used both of water baptism and the baptism of the Holy Spirit. On Pentecost, the wind and sound filled the room, but the actual baptism of the Spirit took place in the form of tongues of fire, which descended upon the disciples. The tongues of fire have more of a resemblance to the pouring of water than immersion. Therefore, as far as the meaning of the word *baptizein* is concerned, those pedobaptists are right who explain that " 'baptize' means to *apply water* by washing, pouring, sprinkling, or immersing." [7] I repeat, it is a historical fact that the Greek words *baptein* and *baptizein* were used in the time of Christ and the apostles in these various meanings among the Greek-speaking Jews and Christians. The command to baptize, therefore, does not in itself show in what manner water should be applied in this rite. True, baptism was usually performed by immersion, but the words of Christ in the institution, twenty-eighth chapter of Matthew, twentieth verse, nevertheless, did not contain a command that it should be done this way, since the word *baptizein* also was used of other kinds of water application. [8]

John: I have to withdraw my assertion that the word *baptizein* always and without exception means to immerse. I admit that the examples you gave show that it was used of other kinds of sacred cleansings too.

Those who defend baptism by sprinkling or pouring usually explain that there was not enough water in Jerusalem for immersing thousands of people. They also say that there was no opportunity to immerse the Ethiopian eunuch, described in the eighth chapter of Acts. Hiscox shows that, according to reliable authorities, the various pools of Jerusalem were quite adequate for such immersions. For instance, the pool of Bethesda alone was three hundred and sixty feet long and one hundred and thirty feet wide. The pool of Siloam was fifty-three feet long and eighteen feet wide. In the area where Philip baptized the Ethiopian eunuch "there is a fine stream of water, called Murubbah, deep enough in June to satisfy the utmost wishes of our baptist friends," as Doctor Thomson says. [9] This shows that there was no need to use the emergency form of baptism, namely, pouring water on the head.

Martin: I have a recently published work which gives forty-eight by sixty-eight meters or about two hundred and ten by one hundred and fifty feet as the size of Bethesda, that is considerably less than the dimensions given by Hiscox. But even so, this pool, which was near the temple, was large enough for immersing thousands of people. You are therefore right in saying that the argument of a shortage of water in Jerusalem against immersion is not valid. In Philippi there was a river where the jailer and his family probably were baptized.

We have no argument against the correctness of immersion as a form of baptism. But we are in disagreement concerning the necessity of this form. You think that the correct external mode of baptism is so essential that baptism by sprinkling or pouring is not true baptism. We believe that baptism is valid and should not be repeated when clean water is used in it, and when it is performed in the name of the Father and the Son and the Holy Spirit, or in the name of Jesus.

Church history shows that God has made no distinction between people baptized by immersion, sprinkling or pouring when He has bestowed His spiritual blessings on them. If the external mode of baptism were as essential as you think, I do not see how God would have given His grace and Spirit to any person who has received baptism by sprinkling or pouring. The Greek Orthodox Church has always used immersion, but its spiritual condition seems to be much worse than of many denominations that use sprinkling or pouring. I think this too testifies for the correctness of our view that the outward mode of baptism is not essential.

John: Maybe you are right in thinking that the external mode of baptism is not quite so important as we used to think. I know that there are some antipedobaptists who are not quite as rigid with regard to the mode of baptism as others are. Still I think that immersion is the preferable form, since it was the form ordinarily used by early Christians, and the form recommended by the Protestant reformers.

NOTES

IV. The Mode of Baptism

1. Augustus Hopkins Strong, *Systematic Theology* (5th ed., revised and enlarged; New York: Armstrong and Son, 1896), pp. 522ff. Edward T. Hiscox, *The New Directory for Baptist Churches* (Philadelphia: American Baptist Publication Society, 1894), pp. 389ff.
2. VII.
3. Luther, *On the Babylonian Captivity of the Church*, 1520. Weimar ed., vol. 6, p. 443.
4. Luther, *Treatise on Baptism*, 1519. Weimar ed.
5. *Ibid.*, vol. 5, p. 1.
6. Calvin, *Institutes of the Christian Religion*, trans. John Allen (7th Am. ed., Philadelphia: Presbyterian Board of Christian Education), book IV, ch. XV, sec. xix, p. 599.
7. *Short Explanation of Dr. Martin Luther's Small Catechism* (St. Louis: Concordia Publishing House, 1912), p. 126.
8. The mode of baptism has been recently discussed in the *Lutheran Witness* (Missouri Synod). Certain Lutheran missionaries had followed the desire of some people in the hill regions of Indiana and baptized them by immersion. This had aroused criticism. The editor of the *Lutheran Witness* defended the action of the missionaries. He pointed out that although the Lutheran Church ordinarily uses pouring, it does not reject immersion as wrong. "Testimony is in place over against any inclination to claim that we Lutherans may not baptize by immersion. For that reason it is not out of order here and there occasionally to resort to immersion if so desired." (*Lutheran Witness*, Dec. 11, 1951, p. 409). Carl A. Gieseler wrote in the Jan. 22, 1952 issue of the same paper in favor of the view of the editor, quoting the statement of Luther in his *Treatise on Baptism* cited above. Gieseler commented: "Luther does not mean to say that he considers immersion essential to valid baptism, but from these words we may see that he would not criticize a Lutheran pastor who would use this method if the catechumen or the parents of an infant request immersion." We agree.
9. Hiscox, *op. cit.*, pp. 430-437.

Conclusion

Martin: The question of the mode of baptism is the least important issue between pedobaptists and antipedobaptists. As I have said, a great number of pedobaptists use immersion. The two great issues are the questions of infant baptism and the significance of baptism.

I read recently a pamphlet written in defense of the baptistic view of baptism. The writer said that after reading the books of those who defend infant baptism their theories seemed very plausible and had a certain charm for him, but when he turned from their writings to the word of God he was not able to find the theories in it. "It has seemed to me," he continues, "that they have read their teachings *into* Scripture, not *out* of it; *eisegesis* rather than *exegesis*." [1] I, for my part, must confess that I have had a similar experience, but in the opposite way. The arguments of those who hold the baptistic view have sometimes seemed plausible and had certain charms for me. But when I have studied the word of God I have not found their theories in it. It seems to me that they have read their teachings into the Bible, not out of it. I do not find the baptistic doctrine of baptism in the New Testament; nor have you been able to show it to me. One cannot hold the baptistic view as long as he takes the teachings of the word of God as they are and follows them. Both the New Testament and the history of the Christian Church show incontestably that infant baptism is in harmony with the plain teachings of Jesus and with the practice of the Apostolic and post-Apostolic Church. The first real opposition to infant baptism appeared in the Middle Ages in a few groups of sectarians called Cathari. In the Ancient Church, Tertullian regarded delay of baptism preferable only for some reasons of expediency, and his reasons were based on doctrinal errors. Otherwise there was hardly any opposition to infant baptism for more than a millennium after the birth of the Church.

The gulf of disagreement is still deeper with regard to the meaning of baptism. According to the baptistic view, baptism is an *act of man*, a symbolic rite in which he confesses his faith

---

[1] H. A. Ironside, *Baptism: What Saith the Scripture* (3d ed., 1930), p. 6.

before men after having experienced salvation. We regard it as an *act of God* upon man, a means of grace, which is given for (into) the forgiveness of sins.

The New Testament never speaks of baptism as an act of confession on the part of man. It always speaks of it as a means of grace which is given for the remission of sins, or for washing from sin, and regeneration. This Biblical view was general in the Church for more than a millennium. The baptistic conception was practically unknown until the twelfth century. The teaching of the Church Universal is also seen from the statement of the *Nicene Creed,* accepted by most Christian churches: "I acknowledge one baptism for the remission of sins." The obvious meaning is that baptism is a means through which sins are remitted.

The baptistic doctrine is therefore a relatively late erroneous view which has no foundation in the Scriptures. The outward mode used by those who hold this view is correct, but that merely means that they have the right external form but a wrong meaning, a correct rite without Scriptural content.

When those who hold the baptistic view rebaptize people after their conversion, they do something that is entirely unbiblical, since infant baptism is a true Scriptural baptism, and the validity and efficacy of baptism does not depend on its external mode and the amount of water used in it. The true Biblical baptism is the one that is understood in the sense of the words of Peter: "Repent ye and be baptized every one of you in the name of Jesus Christ into the remission of your sins; and ye shall receive the gift of the Holy Spirit."

A friend of mine told me some time ago of his own experiences with regard to the baptistic baptism. He had received baptism in his infancy, but then he felt that he should be baptized by immersion. This took place several years after his conversion. It seemed to him that the Spirit of God was urging him to take that step, and so he did, desiring to show obedience to God. I asked him what the new baptism meant to him, and what he experienced in it. His answer was that when he had been baptized by immersion he was through with the question, and was not troubled by it any more. His words indicated that he regarded baptism by immersion as an act of obedience, and when he had done it he felt satisfaction, as a person always feels satisfaction after doing what he understands as the will of God.

The case of this friend of mine has revealed to me more clearly than before that the baptistic baptism is not a New Testament baptism. It is just a work of man. People who receive it do not view it as a baptism into the forgiveness of sins and as a means of grace, an act of God on them. They see it as their own act, and when they have received it they are through with it. Such a view of baptism is entirely unscriptural. We thank God for the baptism into the forgiveness of sins. But we also believe that we are truly saved only if the meaning of baptism has been fulfilled in us in true repentance and faith, in a true knowledge of Christ and obedience to Him.

John: This discussion has been quite an eye opener to me. When we started I thought that I could easily refute your doctrine of baptism. Now at its end I see that it is my conception that has been refuted. I am going to give some more thought and study to these questions, praying that the Lord will help me to understand His truth aright and to follow it.

Martin: May the Lord bless you in that purpose of your heart.

Comparative Summary

I. Infant Baptism

THE BAPTISTIC VIEW

A. Infants should not be baptized because the New Testament contains no command to perform it and never mentions that infants were baptized in the Apostolic Age.

THE PEDOBAPTISTIC VIEW

Jesus teaches that infants should be baptized when He says (1) that infants should be brought to Him and the kingdom of God, being acceptable to it, and (2) that without baptism man cannot enter the kingdom of God and become His disciple.

The Biblical Foundations for these Views

None. Silence is not sufficient proof.

"And they brought unto him also their babes (*brephe*) . . . Jesus called them unto him, saying, Suffer the little children to come unto me, and forbid them not: for of such is the kingdom of God." (Luke 18:15-17)

"Except a man be born of water and the Spirit, he cannot enter into the kingdom of God." (John 3:5)

"Go ye therefore, and make disciples of all nations, baptizing them . . . and teaching them . . ." (Matt. 28:19f)

B. A person should first have a conscious saving faith, and then be baptized. Infants cannot have a saving faith, and therefore should not be baptized.

Infants (*brephe*) receive the kingdom of God, Christ says, and this can be done only by faith. Conscious faith, born in repentance and by hearing the Gospel, was not required by Christ from infants for their reception of the kingdom of God. We should put to them no greater requirements than Jesus did. Adult people must repent and believe before baptism, but a saving faith is not required; penitent faith and prayer for grace suffices.

103

The Biblical Foundations for these Views

None. It has only human rational and psychological assumptions for its foundation.

"Whosoever shall not receive the kingdom of God as a little child, shall in no wise enter therein." (Luke 18:17; Mark 10:15)

"Repent ye, and be baptized every one of you in the name of Jesus Christ unto the remission of your sins . . ." (Acts 2:38)

C. Infant baptism was not practiced in the Apostolic Church, but was introduced by the corrupt Catholic Church.

Infant baptism was practiced in the Apostolic Church, and was in use long before there was any Roman Catholicism.

The Biblical and Historical Foundations for these Views

None. The silence of the New Testament is not sufficient foundation; nor is there any historical foundation.

Infant baptism was generally practiced among the Jews at the time of Christ (proselyte baptism), and He never spoke a word against it. He rather said that infants were acceptable to God's kingdom and received it, and that without baptism no one could enter into this kingdom. Whole families were baptized in the Apostolic Church, just as whole families were taken into the synagogue congregation through baptism. It is quite possible that there were infants in these families, although it cannot be proved. Justin the Martyr, Irenaeus and Tertullian speak of infant and child baptism in the second century, and Origen was baptized in his infancy in A.D. 185 or 186. He, Cyrian, etc., speak of infant baptism as an apostolic and accepted practice in the third century.

II. The Significance of Baptism

A. Baptism is an act of obedience and confession on the part of man, who previously has repented and been saved by faith in the Gospel.

Baptism is a means of grace, and as such an act of grace on the part of God, who imparts His saving grace through it to a lost sinner.

The Biblical and Historical Foundations for these Views

None. Scripture never speaks of baptism as an act of man and confession of faith.

"Baptism doth also now save us." (1 Pet. 3:21)

". . . arise, and be baptized and wash away thy sins, calling on his name." (Acts 22:16)

". . . that he might sanctify it, having cleansed it by the washing of water, with the word." (Eph. 5:26)

"We were buried . . . with him through baptism into death . . ." (Rom. 6:4)

"Be baptized . . . in the name of Jesus Christ unto the remission of your sins . . ." (Acts 2:38)

The Apostolic Church ordinarily baptized penitent sinners, not sinners who already were saved (such cases were exceptional, as in the household of Cornelius).

B. Water cannot wash away sins, only Christ's blood can. Baptism is a symbol of the washing away of sins and of regeneration that has previously taken place.

Baptism has power to wash away sins because Scripture says so, and because the Word is united with the water, and through the Word the blood of Christ.

The Biblical Foundations for these Views

None. The New Testament never speaks of baptism as a mere symbol of previously experienced salvation.

". . . arise, and be baptized, and wash away thy sins," and other New Testament passages quoted in II, A.

III. Mode of Baptism

A. In the time of Christ and the apostles, and for about a millennium after that, baptism was performed by immersion, and only in cases of emergency (sickness, lack of water) was sprinkling or pouring used. The same should be done today.

The baptistic view of the mode of baptism in the Apostolic Church and about a millennium after that is correct.

B. The word *baptizein* in Greek means only and without exception to immerse, dip under water.

The most common meaning of *baptizein* is to immerse, dip under water; but this is not its only meaning; it is used of ceremonial cleansings of various types, also by slight or partial dipping and sprinkling. The commandment to baptize in itself does not therefore show what mode should be used, except that water should be applied in one of these ways.

C. Baptism is a valid and true baptism only when performed by immersion.

Immersion is the preferable form of baptism, but it is valid and equally effective also when performed by sprinkling or pouring, for the main things in it are the promise of the Gospel, the presence of the triune God, and faith, not the amount of water and the external mode.